STATIC

Learn to listen through the noise.
It can save your life.

SALIMA WITT
with Adrienne Moch

One Woman's Story of Surviving
Multiple Near-Death Experiences

STATIC

**Learn to listen through the noise.
It can save your life.**

by Salima Witt

© 2024 Salima Witt
℗ 2024 Kandon Unlimited, Inc.

All rights reserved.
Printed in the United States of America.

No part of this book may be used or reproduced in any mannerwhatsoever without written consent from Salima Witt or Kandon Unlimited, except in the case of brief quotations embodied in critical articles and reviews.

ISBN 13: 978-1735957227
ISBN 10: 1735957224

Dedication

I dedicate this book to my beloved family, whose unwavering love and support have been the cornerstone of my journey.

I also extend this dedication to all those facing adversity. May you find solace and encouragement within these pages.

Table of Contents

Foreword

Introduction

Chapter 1—The Early Years

Chapter 2— Focusing On Zebras

Chapter 3—Oxygen Heals

Chapter 4—Mind Games

Chapter 5—Horsing Around

Chapter 6—Losing Part of Myself

Chapter 7—Brain In Flames

Chapter 8—My Spiritual Awakening

Chapter 9—The Will To Live

Chapter 10—You Are What You Eat

Chapter 11—Lessons Learned And The Road Ahead

Acknowledgments

Foreword

In many areas of the country, one or two entities control all hospital stays. Like all monopolies, these hospitals no longer have any incentive to deliver quality care or most distressing, no desire to treat patients with hard to diagnose illnesses, in Salima's instance. In my forty years at the National Cancer Institute, I cannot count how many heads of many departments had told me if I want to live, stay out of hospitals. Every year, more than 250,000 Americans die of medical malfeasance, mistakes, misinformation, and myths as reported by Johns Hopkins Medical School. This does not include people injured by medical blunders, misdiagnosis, and medication mix-ups or side effects.

The ugly side of mainstream medicine reveals a much larger problem. The medical advice one hears in the mainstream media is often hopelessly outdated or dangerously wrong. The fact that pharmaceutical companies spend six times more money on advertising then on medical research clearly informs you where their interests lie—in the bottom line only. After years of reading about the resolution of long-lasting medical mysteries and attending medical conferences designed for physicians' CME (continuing medical education), it confirms my expertise.

How then is a single individual who has been damaged by healthcare supposed to uncover adequate assistance?

In the decade since my retirement, I have had many discussions with people discarded by mainstream medicine. Almost all of them were ready to take control of their health, often because they are alone and the only ones who can take this responsibility. One of the most interesting medical self-help stories is the subject of this book. Its author, Salima Witt, is one of the most interesting, intelligent, and courageous people I have met. Ever since one of several medical mistakes—leaving part of her placenta in her body causing near-lethal sepsis—she has been extraordinarily aggressive in seeking information and treatments in recovering her health.

Aristotle's admonition that to know oneself is the beginning of all wisdom is particularly difficult from a health perspective when suffering from debilitating illnesses. Physical health involves everything related to your body, beginning with what you put in your mouth or on your body (including what medications you take, drugs kind and dose, and water and alcohol intake). Salima through trial and error found she was hypersensitive to most medications, so she needed to take them alone or in combination at low doses and slowly build up the doses.

Often her symptoms were worsened without any benefit. During the time I have known her, she has gone to many different health professionals and tried many different novel regiments, some of which have helped to reduce the symptoms, some making them worse.

Food intake is an essential health stable itself. It is really difficult to control with all the additives in food before it arrives at your table. Red dye #3 has been banned in the European Union for years, while California just passed a law banning it in food starting in 2027. Food companies that sell a safer food in Europe would not sell it in America; they will only sell the safer product when forced!

Our bodies are 60 percent water and rely on daily hydration. Studies have shown a correlation between dehydration and physical and mental health. Salima is such a healthy good cook, it is a pleasure to be invited to her house for dinner. Poor diet as well as stress, anxiety, and illness can all affect quality and quantity of poor sleep. Poor sleep is associated with a number of mental health conditions and neurodegenerative disorders. Mental health impacts your emotional well-being, including how you talk to yourself and how you handle life's difficulties.

Social health deals with the way we interact with people in our environment. Family relationships are our most important relationships. Fortunately, Salima has the support of two wonderful adult daughters and an adoring husband. Her nuclear family eats dinner together every night. The social aspect of meals is as important as what you are eating. She also has supportive outside friends, particularly those suffering with chronic diseases also. The bottom line is you cannot be physically well unless you are also mentally well and socially well. One needs to address each of these to have a balanced life.

In the time I have known her, Salima has made great progress overcoming the horrendous symptoms she possessed. I trust her spirit will allow her to make progress on this problem. She has made exponential strides and continues to do so.

If we are to win the battle to preserve our personal rights and protect our future family members from the dark forces attempting to make us only commodities, we need courageous people like Salima Witt to continue to pursue remedies to her maladies and speak out concerning how to accomplish this goal.

Dr. Francis W. Ruscetti

Introduction

A beautiful friend of mine told me once when you meet someone who is wise with insight and knowledge, you know they have been through suffering—maybe even long suffering, because it takes suffering, mistakes, and pain to bring wisdom. I have written this book to share the wisdom and insight I've earned through years of long suffering.

We have all heard stories of people miraculously living through Stage 4 cancer, overcoming diagnoses of weeks to live. Without trivializing the magnificence of those achievements, let me tell you that I have been through much more than that. During the course of too many hospital stays to count, I had doctors tell me I would be in a wheelchair for the rest of my life, I would lose one or more of my limbs, I would never be able to live a normal life again—and I was fortunate to be alive.

The latter is definitely true but none of those other prognostications came to pass. I actually had medical professionals tell me I should be dead—or at a minimum catatonic. The particulars are likely to astound you; I've survived a series of life-threatening illnesses when the odds were decidedly against me, time and time again.

I'm not seeking pity and not looking to paint myself as a victim. No way. I decided to write this book because I realized what I learned during all my near-death experiences may help others get through hard times—particularly the fact that for me a gift was reborn as a result of everything I went through. No one goes through life unscathed.

I think perseverance is a trait that deserves more attention. That is what I see as the overarching theme of this book: moving forward despite terrifying obstacles. But how do you do that? My takeaways include gaining an understanding that there is a voice that guides each of us—whether you call it higher self, inner self, intuition, or as I do, God; being my own advocate; focusing on gratitude; and understanding the value of surrender. This book is organized in a way that I hope makes it possible for you to see past all my suffering and frustration and get to the "silver lining."

I truly believe we are all here for a reason. And we all deserve to live the life we choose. It is when the ability to do that is taken away that we can either give up or push through by opening our hearts and minds to new voices and perhaps a new way of living, eliminating the static to listen to what is being told to us.

Salima Witt

Chapter 1

The Early Years

I believe we are all born with an innate gift from God. Some people call it intuition, some higher self and others, like me, simply God. It is more than a sense; it is an ability to direct us out of harm, guide us toward greater purpose, and support us through arduous times. The sheer act of being alive, living through trauma and various experiences, moves us away from the ability to listen to our guide. We are inundated with parental guidelines and constructs, social norms, and the informal rules that govern behaviors in groups, social media, etc. As children, we very rarely are taught to move inward for guidance.

My life has been flooded with traumas and near-fatal experiences that initially removed me completely from my inner guide, God, but eventually brought me full circle to an even greater understanding of it. I believe I was directed back to my guide by everything I went through and ultimately that is what saved my life. I learned how to listen to my intuition and let it guide me.

My story begins in 1972, when I was born in Canada to an immigrant family; my mom was French and my dad was Algerian

Berber. I have one sibling, an older brother. When I was just three years old, I experienced the first trauma of my life—my father left us to go back to Algeria. One day he was there and the next he was gone; I was never told why and was left with a feeling I later learned was ambiguity.

My parents' relationship was tumultuous. They were two people with totally different upbringings—one in the male-dominated North African culture and the other in the more laissez-faire French. This led to great instability in their marriage, and that instability unfortunately trickled down to my brother and me. We each handled our insecure environment in our own way; for me it bred fear and anxiety. I could feel the shaky foundation of our family and it caused me at a very young age to worry excessively.

When my father left, the tiny fragile foundation I did have crumbled. We were left with nothing. We would be eating mustard toast or ketchup on bread for dinners and the fear from my mother was unmistakable. She did not have the skill set necessary to get a good paying job and now was faced with being the sole breadwinner, the provider for herself and two young children.

When I was seven years old, our family moved to the United States, to the Chicago suburb of Skokie. What a change for me! I went from attending a Catholic French school in Montreal to an American public school—and I did not speak English. Although I wasn't held back, I certainly failed at first grade primarily due to the language barrier. Thankfully, due to childhood resilience, my English was far better when I began second grade.

Single mothers were a rarity in those days and mine had to work very hard to provide for my brother and me. I had a lonely upbringing as a result. I knew my mom was doing the best she could but our meager dinners left me never feeling secure about where my next meal was coming from.

I was a latchkey kid. We had no family in the area so I spent most of my time alone and was left to my own devices when it came to putting together my dinner, doing my homework, and showering. I spent a lot of time in nature alone. I had my own tackle box and would fish alone and play with bugs the way other kids played with Barbies. I had those too but I was in my element in nature; I felt connected, alive, and at my best. I felt God there.

I lacked so much peace and security but the times I spent in nature gave me snippets of feeling connected. I was lost in childhood and I yearned for that connection. What I realize now is that our upbringing brings in murkiness to knowing our true inner self because growing up, our environment, which for many of us is chaotic, allows us to absorb so much energy, emotion, and outward stimuli that we lose part of who we really are—our true essence.

I'm not sure I realized I was missing valuable parental guidance but I don't remember being disappointed with my mom; I appreciated her hard work to keep our household afloat even though her despair was often palpable. Many years later, when I became a parent, I vowed to be everything to my children that my mother was not—and fortunately I did not have to struggle financially like she did.

Adding to my feelings of loneliness was the fact that I had no spiritual guidance in my life. I was baptized and only when I was very young did we go to church for holidays. My Christian friends were going to confirmation classes and my Jewish friends to synagogue but faith—which can provide an important foundation—was missing from my life.

I was just eight years old when my grandfather died, an event that coincided with the end of our church visits; there seemed to be a shift in spirituality on my mother's side of the family toward atheism. I remember feeling like the wake was spooky because I was given no explanation about the customs being followed. I was scared and wanted to know what happened to my grandfather. When crying, I asked my aunt where he went and she gave a troubling answer: "He's in a void, just floating in blackness." I don't think I slept for the next two weeks. What an awful thing to say to a child.

The family on my mother's side were all scientists, including microbiologists and chemistry professors, who did not believe in God. So believing in *something*—God, reincarnation, just blind faith—was never instilled in me. Who was God, the bearded guy in the sky I pictured as a child? It didn't make sense to me. I yearned for more of an explanation but didn't know where or how to go about it.

A bit before my grandfather's death, on picture day when I was in second grade, my mom drove me to school. That was a rarity as I usually had to take the bus. I would literally beg my mom for time with her. She worked two jobs and I sometimes wouldn't see her for days. At just six years old, I would make myself dinner and tuck myself into bed on a daily basis. By the time she came home I was fast asleep.

Mom pulled over to the side of the road across from the school to let me out and I ran across the street without looking. I was hit by a car—my head bounced off the windshield and I subsequently was run over. I suffered a severe concussion along with other body aches and pains. This was my first experience with traumatic injury.

Suffering In Silence

While I recovered from my physical wounds after a time, I was left with what I now know was post-traumatic stress disorder (PTSD) caused by trauma—but no one talked about mental health issues like that back then. I didn't adjust well after the accident. I was afraid to cross a street. I obsessed that a car would come by and hit me again; I had visions of that every time I stepped onto a street. Trauma settled in. There was no one to talk to about this; I certainly wasn't going to bare my soul to the aunt who so traumatized me at my grandfather's wake.

My mom forced me to walk across our street to "toughen up" but that episode backfired on her. I remember looking at the curb and looking across the road over what looked like an insurmountable amount of concrete to cross. I wouldn't even attempt to cross a street again for six months.

I began to be introverted, depressed, and anxious when I was a third grader. The combination of my father leaving, moving to a new country, and being hit by a car in just two years was more than I could bear. I ended up ditching third grade for six weeks and was only busted when my brother came home sick from school one day.

We have little control about our start in life. The lesson I learned from what had happened to me and how I processed or perceived it was that I needed to do what was necessary to live through whatever life threw at me. I was under tremendous pressure as a kid. Will we have food and shelter? What if mom lost her job? Would we move back to Canada? There was so much about my life that was unsure—and on top of that was the trauma from the accident—but all my worries were private. I didn't share anything with my mom; she simply didn't have the time. And going to a therapist was simply unheard of.

Although I didn't know it then, I was yearning for nature, as it was the only connection to God. It was the sole time in my life I felt peace and calm. It was as if life around me was filled with static noise like on an AM radio dialing old school through all the channels. But when I sat in nature, a clear, calm, and peaceful station would come in and I would feel peace and harmony within.

I look back and see I was being led but I didn't know why or what was guiding me then. It took decades for me to understand how important tuning in or practicing discernment really is. Back then, I was too young to understand. There was so much chaos outwardly around me that there was a disconnect.

Now I know that we must be conscious of all those outside influences and release ourselves from them to be able to say, "This is not my authentic self. I'm not going to own what is not mine to own. This is not me—this is the product of things that happened around me."

When we reflect back on our childhoods, we need to ask ourselves some important questions: Where did I feel peace? Where did I feel joy? With a relative, what would I do? Reconnect for a moment to what was authentically peaceful and joyful.

An important part of the work we must do as we grow older is to realize consciously that a lot of the angst and neuroses we are plagued with as adults don't come from us at all. When we are cognizant of this we can begin to let go and set free the traumas we inherited. They are not our authentic self. They are experiences we had no control of; they are not you. We must ask ourselves am I reacting to this situation as my ten-year-old self with no coping skills or am I reacting to this situation as a grown adult with life experience? Sometimes our initial reaction to a difficult situation is the most maladjusted reaction from the gut, from when we were young—a knee-jerk reaction that is not best suited for you. It takes mindfulness to ask am I doing this? Is this young me or me now? Regain strength by letting go of the trauma and saying, "I am more than what I experienced. I am older now, wiser now and I have the ability to control how I react to an experience and pay attention to my thoughts and feelings." Begin to go inward.

Looking back, I realize my childhood experiences were framed by feeling my mother's anxiety and her perception of an unsure world. I didn't know how to separate her experiences from mine but I was instilled with a sense of perseverance that I would need to draw from over and over again as an adult.

The Cantaloupe Cyst

The chaos in my upbringing continued in my teenage years. Being reared by a single mother took its toll on me. My mother didn't have much time for my needs, so consequently I didn't pay attention to my needs either.

When I was seventeen, out of nowhere I started feeling pressure in my lower abdomen and I had to pee all the time. My mom took me to the doctor, who suspected a urinary tract infection (UTI) but the test came back negative. Days later, I went back to the doctor because I simply could not function, had some more tests run, and learned I needed emergency surgery to remove what turned out to be an ovarian cyst the size of a cantaloupe—ten pounds! The ovary in which it had formed also needed to be removed.

This was way before the days of minimally invasive robotic surgeries. I had a staples running from my pubic bone almost to my ribs and was in the hospital for three weeks. It took me two more months to recover fully at home and I was left with a twenty-inch scar. I remember that time as a whirlwind and my biggest concern being that I'd be "marked" forever. We're so resilient when we're young, never really thinking about the bigger picture.

My surgery happened in June and in August I was put on birth control pills to help conserve my remaining ovary. Life went on—but

I was concerned about the *why*. What did I do to contribute to this? Why did this happen to me? No one had answers other than "this happens sometimes." But in my gut I knew something contributed to it but I just didn't know what. Things like this don't "just happen."

I was just a teenager but asking questions the medical community had no answers to. Was this cyst a product of a traumatic upbringing? Was it due to my diet, my environment, or my genetic makeup? No one knew. As I was maturing to young adulthood I felt even more lost than I did as a child. I had no faith. I felt bombarded by the outside world. I felt beat up by the world. I had zero confidence in my abilities. The pressures of leaving home and making money were looming. Little did I know that God was about to throw me the most beautiful gift—the gift of love.

Meeting My Anchor

Years later, when I was twenty-two, I had a full-time job, I went to school, and in my "spare" time I worked for a photographer painting backgrounds on muslin for photo shoots. (Photoshop was many years away!) In the midst of a brutal Chicago winter, I had a weekend painting job in North Dakota that was going to pay $1,000.

I got out to O'Hare Airport on Friday only to learn my flight had been canceled. I raced to another gate to try to get on another flight only to find there was just one seat available—and I overheard an elderly couple discussing whether one of them should take the seat or they should wait to travel together. I so wanted to get on that plane—$1,000 was a big payday for me—that I did something that was so out of character for me: I interjected and told the couple I'd solve their problem by taking the seat. They agreed so I got on the flight.

I started talking with the attractive young guy who was sitting next to me. He was nineteen, about two and a half years younger than me, and said he was a student at the University of Maryland who was traveling to see his dad, who'd had a stroke. After I told him I was originally from Canada and he said he was too, I said "yeah, sure" but he showed me his passport showing Humboldt, Saskatchewan, as his place of birth. I thought, "oh, he really is from Canada." That was interesting so we talked a lot about our native land.

We discovered we had plenty of other things in common—a love of nature, fishing, and hiking; being loners growing up; and the same fundamentals. By the time we landed in North Dakota we'd exchanged phone numbers. About a week later, after we had both returned to our respective homes, he called and we continued to keep in touch. We talked for months, enjoying each other's company. Remember back then there was dial-up internet; no one searched for people online as they do now.

I really liked this guy—Brendan—but I was starting to feel a little perplexed about him. I thought something was amiss after I learned he lived in a four-bedroom house by himself and he told me about his travels, which included snowboarding trips and going down to Florida to golf with some buddies. He was a student? I wondered if he was wealthy but that didn't jive with his mom being a nurse. Was he a drug dealer? Things weren't adding up for me but I was raised not to ask intrusive personal questions so I didn't. I did keep mental notes. (And remember, googling was not an option back then.)

When the opportunity for me to attend a photo convention in Baltimore came up, I called Brendan and asked if I could see him. After a rather uncomfortable pause, he said he'd call me back. Uh-oh. This is when the other shoe was going to drop.

He began the conversation by saying, "I have something to tell you." That is never good. Then he goes on to say he lied to me. He's not in school. (Looking back—his studies never came up!) He said he plays in the NHL; he's a professional hockey player. What?! I was blindsided, and interestingly my innate gut reaction was mild disgust.

"Oh no. You're one of those guys!" I was thrown for a loop because I was appalled by cocky athletes and disappointed to say the least. But he was quick with a response: "This is why I didn't tell you." He went on to explain that he knew on the plane he liked me—he'd noticed me in the gate area and was thrilled when I ended up seated right next to him. If all he'd wanted was a "bootie call," he'd have come clean right away but he didn't want me to like him because he was a professional athlete nor did he want me to be repelled, thinking he was one of "those guys."

It was too much to process right away. It took me about two weeks to work through this huge news. I considered professional athletes to be revolting and full of themselves—and knew they always had women throwing themselves at them. But after some processing, I became thankful for his subterfuge. It would have been overwhelming to know what he did professionally upfront. Would I have been myself? Would I have tried to impress him? His was a world I had no context of—money, fame, fast living. I was overwhelmed to say the least. But since Brendan and I had already established a bond, I flew east to see him.

When I saw him at the gate, I was so thankful I agreed to come. There was this tranquility about him—being around him gave me the same feelings I had when I was in nature. He had a stoic, calm, confident demeanor—the exact opposite of me. It was something I had never felt with anyone. I felt safe in his strength, and I don't mean in his physical strength. Brendan has always had a strong personal conviction about him and it was something I was drawn toward.

As we spent time together, there was a connection I'd never felt before. For the first time in my life, I felt a respite from chaos. The man I knew was going to be my husband and the life he provided was the exact opposite of what I'd experienced so far in life—what I had yearned for. I basked in the peace, tranquility, and security he represented—all things I'd never had but wanted so badly growing up.

But I had a learning curve to traverse and it started almost the moment I got off the plane on that first visit. Brendan said he had a prior professional engagement, an autograph session at Dick's Sporting Goods featuring him and Rafael Palmeiro, who was playing for the Orioles. It was so foreign to me. I walked around the mall and then returned to see a long line, women having their breasts exposed to be autographed, and some asking Brendan what he was doing later. It was just like what I had imagined. I felt uneasy and rather inadequate but hung with it because I knew there was something special between us.

The world of a professional athlete is different. They don't have to search for women to date because women do throw themselves at them. They have to keep a real level head to ensure their ego doesn't get huge. I saw Brendan handled it well. Most of them don't handle it well at all; there is much more cheating in professional sports than monogamy.

I was naive but Brendan had seen the world—he had more radar and was a rock after leaving home at fourteen to pursue his dream of playing hockey as a career.

A Slow Progression—and A Surprise

Brendan and I were both seeing other people when we met and we didn't live in the same place—me in Chicago and him in Maryland—so our relationship progressed rather slowly, starting as a great friendship. During hockey season Brendan was focused on his career and in the summer he went back to Canada to spend time with family. We would see each other in between for short trips when we could. It wasn't until the end of 1997 that we got more serious, and after being together during the Olympic break in 1998 we made plans for me to move in with him in Annapolis. That happened in April.

While I knew I loved Brendan, the transition was hard for me. I left everything I had and knew no one there except him. We got engaged just two months after I moved in and a month after that we received some rather earth-shattering news.

I started feeling a little sick to my stomach. Remember, I had only one ovary—so I ovulated every other month—and I was on birth control to help ensure that ovary remained viable. My doctor had said it might take years for me to get pregnant. Knowing that, I went off the pill but when my symptoms occurred just a month later, it never dawned on me initially that I could be pregnant. But I was; we were expecting a baby.

While I was thrilled at the prospect of becoming a mom, my dysfunctional childhood reared its ugly head as I was absolutely unprepared for what was to come. In my world, no one ever talked about it if someone was ill or struggling; I was raised with a "you're on your own" mentality. I got some help from other hockey wives but I really didn't do too much planning because I didn't know what I was supposed to do.

I had no idea where to begin. It was so foreign; I didn't even know what baby stuff I needed to buy. None of my girlfriends back home were pregnant yet so I couldn't rely on them for any firsthand knowledge. But looking back I did trust part of my intuition and got through it.

Thankfully, the birth of my daughter Aliana was fairly uneventful and Brendan I were excited to be parents. But you know what no one ever tells you about giving birth? You feel physically awful after it. You're sitting in a sitz bath with stitches in your vagina, it's painful to poop, and you get no sleep. Then in my case, I didn't have any family close by to provide support so I was alone after Brendan left for a four-day road trip right after we took our bundle of joy home.

My pro athlete husband was playing in another city; many new mothers face similar challenges—military deployments happen and doctors are on call. It's unusual for them to be aware that they are regular people and not "gods." Athletes in particular are told from a young age that they're special, gifted—and then they're thrown into a world where they're given everything they want; everyone is at their beck and call.

I knew from the start that Brendan had to concentrate on hockey because it takes a lot of focus. This may sound politically incorrect these days but I stand by it even today—when one partner is going 110 percent with their occupation it is not a fair distribution of responsibilities in a marriage to also ask them to take on 50 percent of raising an infant. In the sports world, it would be unheard of and Brendan's performance would suffer as a result. He was supporting our family. I never resented what he needed to do to stay at the top of his game.

Once Aliana was born I had a complete life change. I made her my number one priority—all my energy went to loving her and keeping my family happy, thriving, and intact. I focused on the well-being of my husband and daughter—and myself—as a full-time job. I remember when Brendan would play there is what they call the pregame meal; it is a protein/carb meal players eat before each game around lunchtime. When he had home games, I would be sure to be home to make him his meal, filled with nutritious ingredients.

I remember sharing this with one of the other hockey wives and she thought I was crazy. "Why would you do that?" she said. "He's going to expect that every game day." I looked at it another way—I really enjoyed our lunches together. It's no big surprise that couple eventually divorced. As a matter of fact, Brendan and I are the exception when it comes to making it for the long term; most of the couples we knew during his playing days have split up.

Given how I was raised, I had very little trust in my abilities and was anxious and filled with doubt. But I persevered and began to gain confidence; I knew I didn't want Aliana to have a childhood like mine.

With our baby girl in tow, Brendan and I got married on July 16, 1999, in Maui. We agreed on a small wedding, with the only attendees being our immediate families and best friends. We spent two weeks in paradise.

Looking back, I think we may not have gotten together if Brendan had told me right away what he did for a living. I'm not sure I would have overcome my preconceived notions about professional athletes—which I have since learned are correct for many of them!

Many years into our marriage, Brendan added an anchor to his many tattoos—signifying his role as my anchor time after time after time.

Since Brendan and I both came from two-children families, we knew we would eventually try for baby number two. Eventually ended up being the end of 2001—and wouldn't you know, on our very first try our daughter Safiya was conceived. She was born in September 2002.

I was planning to get my tubes tied at her birth but things didn't go as smoothly as they had when Aliana came into the world. I didn't know it at the time but I was starting on a long, long journey, complete with many twists and turns, that would test my ability to overcome a succession of health conditions that are often fatal.

#1 Witt's Its

- We have little control about our start in life.

- Our upbringing brings in murkiness to knowing our true inner self because growing up, our environment, which for many of us is chaotic, allows us to absorb so much energy, emotion, and outward stimuli that we lose part of who we really are—our true essence.

- A big part of the work we have to do as we grow older is to realize that a lot of our neuroses and issues—things that plague us—don't really come from us at all.

- We must be conscious of all the outside influences and release ourselves from them to be able to say, "This is not my authentic self. I'm not going to own what is not mine to own. This is not me—this is the product of things that happened around me."

Chapter 2

Focusing On Zebras

The birth of a child is a miraculous event. I'd had an uneventful delivery for our first daughter and was looking forward to the same for number two. But things turned out a bit differently.

I had an unremarkable pregnancy and the second time around I did have a support system of friends. This was 2002 and Brendan was at the height of his career. He had a long road trip scheduled around my due date of September 14 so we made the decision to induce if I hadn't gone into labor by then.

That ended up being what happened, so with a little help from oxytocin, I had a beautiful delivery. It went perfectly; I only had to push twice and there she was. All seemed fine until about a half an hour later, when I told the nurse I felt weak. She attributed it to my hormones being stressed from the birth and suggested Brendan leave to get me something to eat, so he did.

About ten minutes after he left, with the baby in my hands, I had just enough time to tell the nurse I didn't feel well before I lost consciousness. I saw stars, my arms buckled, and everything went black. The nurse grabbed the baby and for I don't know how long I was in and out of consciousness. I recall hearing some of the emergency orders—"bleeder, hemorrhaging"—and felt needles going into my legs that I later learned were injecting drugs into my system to try to stop the bleeding.

I remember feeling a waterfall come out of me and I started to lose my ability to hear anything. The nurses continued to inject me and connected me to an IV. Meanwhile, I had lost the ability to understand anything. Complete confusion surrounded me.

I lost a lot of blood. My hematocrit—the percentage by volume of red cells in the blood—was dangerously low. The normal range for adult females is 36 percent to 44 percent and mine was just 15.5 percent. All signs pointed to me needing a transfusion but that didn't happen.

I laid there unable to talk. The weakness was overwhelming. When Brendan returned with a hamburger he saw his wife covered in blood and incoherent. He was scared to death. They told him they believed I had a hemorrhage and decided to keep me in the hospital for tests.

The Obvious Is Ignored

I was barely stable and could hardly walk or understand language—let alone take care of a newborn. Despite the fact that I was dizzy and couldn't think straight, I was deemed stable enough to be released after being in the hospital for three days. I couldn't drive and could barely take care of the kids. Remember, Brendan was gone on his road trip. Thankfully, I'd set up a night nurse before any of this happened since I knew I'd be alone with a newborn and a three-year-old. She ended up staying with us for six months, for twelve hours a day. My mom also came to help.

A week went by and I wasn't feeling any better. I felt like a quarter of a human being. Life was happening around me but I felt like I was just floating, so depleted. Then I had a bizarre dream where I was buried in snow and so cold. I woke up shivering with a 103-degree fever. I called my internist but didn't get a call back. I was getting rigors (uncontrollable shakes) and even though my mom kept saying I'd be okay, I knew I needed help.

My temperature kept rising; by midday it was 104. I had to make a decision. I drove myself to the ER, feeling a constant sense of dread. I walked in, got to the desk, and fell unconscious. When I awoke I was in triage on the OBGYN floor where I'd so recently given birth. The doctors were trying to figure out what was wrong with me as my fever kept climbing. Was it the West Nile virus? Lyme disease? Mediterranean fever? They never even considered that what was happening had anything to do with my pregnancy since I had delivered just days prior.

Establishing The Fight

As the doctors continued to try to identify what was happening to me, I had a temperature of 105 degrees and a low white blood count, which could interfere with my body's ability to fight infection.

I had an ultrasound that showed something large—the size of a grapefruit—that they thought was a blood clot. They still failed to connect what was happening to me to the fact that I had so recently given birth.

Without alarm, I truly thought I was going to die. I called Brendan, who was in Texas, to say goodbye to him. I told him my fever kept climbing, I was uncontrollably shaking and going in and out of consciousness. There was a presence, a heaviness in my breath. I felt my essence slipping away. He got on the first flight home in the middle of the night but by the time he arrived at the hospital I wasn't conscious. I had fallen into a coma.

The night before, I recall feeling like I could go into a deep sleep; it was like nothing I had felt before in my life. It was like the way you feel after being given propofol before surgery, an extreme heaviness you cannot fight. I felt I would not come out of it if I succumbed. Mentally, the fight was established. I wanted to do all I could to live.

As the medical professionals were wrestling with all types of reasons why I was this way, they finally called in an infectious disease specialist to consult. She immediately said my symptoms were related to my daughter's birth. It was a blood issue—and she ordered blood tests and cultures. There it was. E. coli septic shock. I was put on a Cipro drip pic line. During that time I experienced tachycardia—a rapid heartbeat (220 beats per minute when a typical heart rate is from 60 to 100)—and my blood pressure hovered at a very dangerous 50/30.

When I finally woke up, feeling extremely weak, I had no concept of what happened. I was scared and confused but there he was—Brendan—next to the bed by my side, holding my hand. Tears were rolling down my face as I asked him what happened. Was I okay?

I learned that in addition to being diagnosed with E. coli septic shock, I was suffering from hypovolemic shock, leukopenia, and adrenal gland and kidney issues. I was seriously, seriously ill; the mortality rate for those with E. coli septic shock is 50 percent and when you add in hypovolemic shock it rises to 80 percent. It was against all odds to survive this.

I also was anemic; my ferritin level was 3 when the normal range is 11 to 150. It was overwhelming to say the least. But I was a warrior. I stayed in the hospital for a few weeks and when I was deemed "stable" I went home, tethered to IV medication. I could barely walk. I was still bleeding so much and even passed a clot the size of a softball. I was thankful that Brendan's mother, a midwife, was there to help me.

Because I still felt so weak and like I was not progressing, over the next six weeks I went back to the hospital three times. The first time I went to the emergency room I was told I had depression and it was all in my head. The second time the diagnosis was acid reflux. Then on the third visit I was diagnosed with other psychiatric ailments despite the fact that I was still bleeding heavily. I was so weak. Just the act of getting in the car to go to the emergency room was exhausting.

I had no more energy to waste on these fruitless visits. I was slipping backward, with less and less ability to live. My inner voice told me not to return to the same hospital multiple times—the hospital that nearly killed me—but I did it anyway because I was full of fear and dread.

Ultimately, I returned to the ER of hospital where I delivered and the OBGYN who brought our second daughter into the world met us there. Brendan had some stern words for him, to put it kindly. He lost it and yelled at the doctor that he "better fix my wife."

On October 30, they finally did another ultrasound and found—whoops!—that what they had seen earlier in my uterus had never gone away; what they thought was a clot was a grapefruit-sized piece of retained placenta. That was the cause of my raging infection—necrotic (dead) tissue had been sitting there in my uterus, festering inside me for six weeks. Depression, huh? That's what the medical industry told me in the emergency room two weeks before.

I went through a dilation and curettage (D&C), after which the bleeding stopped but I still really couldn't function. I was mostly homebound; I felt weak, had no energy, and couldn't think straight.

I did know I was lucky to be alive but I didn't feel like I was doing much living. I continued to not be progressing; I was deteriorating. After the holidays, I went back to the doctor who had delivered my first daughter, someone who had forty years of medical experience. He had never heard of what had happened to me. I clearly recall him telling me this was gynecology 101, so he had a difficult time grasping the malpractice. He was concerned that the necrotic tissue being there for so long could have caused irreparable injury and I might lose my uterus. He recommended exploratory surgery to see what was going on and asked me to give him carte blanche based on what he saw. I trusted him and was in such need of experienced help that I said yes.

From the moment I woke up I felt different. Turns out he had removed all the necrotic tissue from my uterus in what was deemed an invasive D&C. I truly believe he saved me. Fully six months after giving birth I started lactating. That's not supposed to happen. Weird things were going on in my body. I had a long road ahead of me. I had so much pain. My body ached every single day forward. I vowed to push through the pain as I slowly saw improvements every day, although I had severe deficits in my body.

Due to Brendan being a pro athlete, a reporter from the *Washington Post* wrote an article about what we'd gone through, "I'm Just So Happy to Be Alive," which appeared in the paper on September 11, 2003.

Getting "Me" Back

It was not until the summer that I could start functioning like a normal person. I'd lost a tremendous amount of blood and had a raging septic infection that went unchecked for so long—so the damage was widespread. I was so frustrated after going to doctors when I was in so much pain only to be told they had no answers for me. When my internist admitted he didn't know how to treat me, he referred me to his doctor, who said something rather sobering to Brendan: "Don't think what she went through won't scar her for life."

For over a year I felt like I lived in a fishbowl, like I was going through life with my hands over my ears. I couldn't tell where sounds were coming from or what people were saying; it all sounded like white noise so I learned to read lips. I was like a jigsaw puzzle that needed to be put together; it was like cleaning up wreckage after a storm.

As different health problems came up from the aftermath of septic shock—such as an issue with my kidneys when my white blood count was dangerously low and when a pituitary infarction caused all the hair on my body to fall out—I had to take things one step at a time. I hated being sickly because it truly wreaked devastation on my family. I was constantly going to doctors. It was quite traumatic for all of us to realize my illnesses took a toll on everyone, even my poor children. I could see the toll on both my little ones, especially Aliana. She began acting out, which was her way to deal with the stress of it all. Plus, because Brendan was in the prime of his career and I didn't want him to have to constantly worry about me—I put pressure on myself to get better. I vowed to push as hard as I could. My husband had worked his whole life to be at the pinnacle of professional hockey and I didn't want him to worry one bit about me anymore.

I lost so much during that time. My quality of life was stolen from me since I didn't have the ability to walk or hear properly, or even the energy to bond with my children. I once had a normal existence—a somewhat physical existence—but that was in the past. I did as much as I could but now I was tethered to a bed half of the day because I couldn't fathom having the strength to manage an entire day. It was all taken away from me.

Another casualty was a horse Brendan had bought for me. I'd loved horses since I was a child and while we didn't have money for me to pursue that interest, I worked eight hours at a local stable every Sunday when I was twelve years old in exchange for horseback riding lessons. Imagine my joy when many years later I was gifted with my own horse and my despair when we had to sell him after I became sick. Think of how you would feel to see your dreams coming true—and then you were literally fighting for your life.

Years later, I was recounting my post-birth experience to a doctor who was wiser than those who attended me that day. He asked me, "What do you think of when you hear hooves galloping?" "Horses," I quickly replied. Well, he sadly said, your doctors were thinking of zebras. They discounted the obvious to wildly speculate on what might be wrong.

You simply don't go through something like this unscarred psychologically. It was really more than I could bear. I had physical scars reminding me daily of what ran through my veins—not to mention what it did to my brain and psyche. How did I survive? Why did I survive? I had flashbacks; images of dying or losing consciousness raged through me.

Psychotherapy is not for everyone and it took me several tries to find someone I felt connected with me. I remember I went to a therapist in Annapolis, Maryland, who literally fell asleep during our session. I walked out. It takes time to find someone you bond with and can trust. After I finally did, we slowly untangled the trauma, which was not a pretty process. There are layers to get through—getting hit by a car, my father leaving, abandonment, being near death—peeling the onion so to speak. Those experiences are never really gone. When you live through them, you learn they are a part of you; they are your history. You earned the scars. You survived. You are stronger than you realize. God gives you his strength but you have to listen to realize that—and I had not yet gained that understanding.

The Need To Tune In

In our youth and young adulthood, we learned from our parents, from people we look up to—our elders—and we also learned from our mistakes. We are all told we have a voice inside us, our gut instinct, our intuition, right? What is intuition? When we say, "Aha! That's my gut feeling and I'm going with it," what is the feeling we feel? It's an energy, is it not?

Intuition is a manmade word. Is it a feeling? Is it a sense? And if so, what is guiding this sense? Who is to say man has the knowledge to answer those questions. We simply don't. Maybe it's not a sense at all. Maybe it's our higher selves, or God. It has only our best interest at heart, does it not? It's love and light and guidance. Is that not God? Isn't God love? Why is it when we do not pay attention and listen to that feeling we have regret? Everyone seems to have a thought about it. I believe it to be God. I will explain further as we go on.

I realized my ability to tune into my intuition or God was very murky at best at this time of my life. After all the trauma I had survived as a child, I very rarely listened to myself and certainly did not give myself grace. Having been raised with so much doubt gave way to a childhood and young adulthood driven not by this inner guide but by fear.

I have come to learn it is impossible to listen to our inner guide when we are being directed by fear. My experience in the hospital and the constant rejection of my input—being told it was all in my head—was one of the first times as a young adult when I realized I was being guided in the wrong direction—not listening and paying attention.

Starting To Take Charge

But I was becoming a different person, someone who would not blindly give authority to medical personnel again, or anyone for that matter. I realized I didn't have the tools to go through adversity based on how I was raised; I didn't give my inner voice the authority I should have—but I started listening to it more. Now when I feel there's something wrong, I see more clearly where to go for help.

How do you do this? How do you tune in? When I fell ill I spent a lot of time alone. I gained a perspective I never saw before. When I sat there alone in quiet I took a conscious and mindful look at what was going on inside my head and then throughout my whole body. I watched my thoughts, my wants, and my fears like I was an observer. I felt and paid attention to where I would hold tension—in my neck, my heart, all over my body. This was the first time in my adult life I realized I was guiding my perceptions of life, not through a greater power but through my own wants and thoughts. My existence was guided by what I had experienced and all the thoughts that accompanied it.

When I came to this conclusion, I thought what happens when I just observe, let it all go to God, a greater power than me. I was the sole controlling conductor of my experiences in my life—at least, I thought I was. I gained an understanding that when I let go there was a whole other layer I didn't tap into my existence—my guide, my intuition, my higher self, God. People call this knowing something more profound, greater than self, that as an observer you see and feel more when you deconstruct in prayer or meditation. It's a profound sense of connection without a wish for the direction a thought gives or a desire but a true sense of what is best for you.

It was the beginning of disentangling the interference going on inside of me—the static.

I have come to appreciate the importance of the inner self—when you sit with yourself to gain clarity and tune into your personal radio station loud and clear. It provides a guide that lets you know what path to take. As a result of the instability of my youth, my radio station was staticky at best.

During illness, during absolute physical illness when we are in dreadful pain and suffering, it is extremely difficult to hear your guide. Your station becomes harder to find since things are more stressful and you have less time to meditate and pray and more fright and trepidation. But the more you listen, it comes in deeper and deeper, clearer and clearer, and it can mitigate your fear. As I fought to take control of what was happening to me, it was the first time I tuned into God and received the clear guidance I really needed. God was talking and I was listening. It would definitely not be the last time I had to call on His guidance to help me persevere.

#2 Witt's Its

- Having an extremely traumatic life event, a catastrophic near-death event, can result in dark inner chaos to take hold.

- A faint voice may speak to you but you may barely hear it—and that affects your decision-making.

- My inner voice told me not to return to the same hospital six times—the hospital that nearly killed me—but I did it anyway because I was full of fear, dread, and dark energy.

- The truth is not always easy to hear; low vibrational fear and anger can take hold over the voice that talks to you with love and light.

- During illness, during absolute physical illness when we are in dreadful pain and suffering, it is extremely difficult to hear that voice.

Chapter 3

Oxygen Heals

As I began the journey toward regaining my health, I was still dealing with comorbidities. I had trouble understanding sounds—I couldn't tell their direction, where they were coming from—and I had dreadful balance issues. I was told it was CAPD (Central Auditory Process Disorder). This is what allopathic medicine called it; I called it residue from almost dying. I was still having issues with my adrenal glands not working too well and my body hurt all over. It felt like I had aged thirty years. My immune system was shot; if I cut my finger it would get infected and if someone around me got sick I would get it ten times worse. I also wasn't dealing well with the cold—and I'm a native Canadian!—so when Brendan's season was over in 2004 we decided to go to Florida, where there would be plenty of heat and natural Vitamin D.

We traveled to Jupiter in the Sunshine State and had a wonderful time. Brendan loved to surf, the kids loved the beach, and I loved the fact that I just felt more comfortable—my body hurt less. We'd planned to be there for a week but three days in Brendan and I looked at each other and said, "why don't we live here?"

Two days later we bought a house. Yeah, I know. Wow. While I really wouldn't suggest this for most people, it worked for us. We felt like life is short. Death comes like a thief in the night, quick and unexpected. That mindset helped us both come to decisions easier. There was an understanding to live life to the fullest. On June 4, 2004, we became Floridians. But knowing ourselves we knew there would eventually be somewhere else we called home. We loved seeing the world and experiencing new surroundings.

When we decided to make the move, we had a pretty good idea a lockout would happen in the NHL that fall—and it did. We sold our house in Maryland when it became official.

The lockout came at the high point of Brendan's career. You cannot just stop playing competitive hockey for a year and still be at the height of your game. We saw many NHL players take positions on European teams while things were in the air regarding the 2004 season.

Professional sports is a lot like the military but of course with a higher salary. There is a lot of moving involved and as a mother and wife you have to acclimate to change. So we lived "across the pond" for three months to ensure Brendan could stay in shape. He played for the Bracknell Bees in England and we all enjoyed our time there.

Back in Florida, I was starting to heal. My stamina was coming back and I was getting therapy for my CAPD. My issues were becoming tolerable. I continued to have leukopenia, and I dealt with that the best I could. My kids were at a wonderful school, and it was there I made a friend (another mom) who was also an equestrian. She had horses and she invited me to Wellington, the equestrian mecca of the US just thirty minutes from where we lived, for a competition. I was trepidatious but decided to go—and it was amazing.

The smells, the sounds, being in my element again brought me so much joy. I got back on a horse but a lot had changed. I had balance issues and had to compensate for them. I was thankful I was once again able to ride. Many would say that was not a wise decision, being it is a dangerous sport. What do you do? I felt alive again. Being near horses—their smell, their sounds, the connection you feel when you are riding—it had been something I had known since I was ten years old. Despite the obvious risks I pushed on. One month later I bought a horse and started training and competing in Wellington.

Life finally got back to normal for me. In addition to being able to enjoy riding horses, I volunteered at the Palm Beach Zoo working with the primates I love so much, and even traveled around the world. I had four to five years that were really lovely; with only having mild health issues I felt normal, whatever that means! These were the quiet years of my life; I focused on raising my children and supporting Brendan's life and career—enjoying every minute. While I always had some health problems, they were not what I considered problematic—aches and pains that didn't stop me from living.

I knew from firsthand experience that when you can't live life that's all you want to do. And I also came to know that it's easy to be so thankful to be alive—and perhaps too fragile and breakable—that you don't journey inward.

A New Problem

In the fall of 2010, I started to feel bad again. Following my sepsis-induced coma, I had continual pain in my joints that never went away but I'd dealt with it over the years. Literally overnight the pain became intolerable, and a new, unbearable pain came over my arms and legs, reverberating from the long bones of my arms and the long bones of my legs. I couldn't lift my arms over my head; it was as if they were so heavy, with weights on them, making that simple movement impossible. My legs felt as if they would buckle when I walked. I had trouble even functioning—and burning, searing pain in my bones. The only way I can describe it is it was like being repeatedly struck with hot bolts of lightning.

Back to the doctor I went. No one knew what was wrong with me. Not this again. But the tests I took excluded everything—they all came back normal, even thirteen MRIs. My chiropractor threw everything but the kitchen sink at my problem but couldn't figure it out. Neither could a neurologist. I had to cancel a trip we'd planned overseas. Sometimes I was in so much pain that I retreated to the laundry room to cry because I didn't want my kids to see me falling apart. I'd never had that kind of pain before but I endured it because I didn't want to take painkillers; for me, they came with worse side effects than just dealing with the pain.

We entrust doctors, people with white coats, to know what's best for us. Be mindful that this is not true most of the time. You go to them thinking they will know what ailment you have and voilà—all better. For me this was almost never the case. For every ten doctors I saw maybe one would have answer.

Being told over and over again by medical professionals that they couldn't find a reason for my suffering was wearing on me. It was like déjà vu. Some days I almost started believing I was crazy but I knew I couldn't go there or I'd be dead. Despite wanting to be strong, the constant "no's" played on my insecurities. Was I just a wimp? Maybe it was psychosomatic; maybe those who said that were right. Could I really be this messed up in the head that I created all this agonizing pain? But at the bottom of my heart, I knew it was up to me to choose what thoughts and feelings I gave authority to.

By the grace of God, a friend—I call her my guardian angel—introduced me to a seasoned rheumatologist. This was a new specialty for me. I had never been to a rheumatologist before. I began a series of blood tests I had never had before—ANA, Complement C4, immunoglobulins, and much more—to measure the amount of C4 proteins, antinuclear antibodies, and other antibodies in my blood. Fortunately, this rheumatologist was a cut above all the bad doctors and guessers I'd been dealing with. He was the head of rheumatology at Good Samaritan in Palm Beach and very experienced—seventy years old and still practicing. He immediately said I didn't have an autoimmune condition, which had been the prevailing opinion.

He ran a battery of tests and then called me into his office, where he shared the MRI images with me and pointed out these spots all over my bones. He believed they were microinfarcts in my long bones, the result of the death of bone tissue in both of my arms and both of my legs from the septic shock. He also believed my coma and septic shock caused the minimal amount of blood I had at the time to pool to my organs to keep me alive—causing the bones not to have enough blood supply for days so they started dying off. He said many if not most people who endured what I did ended up losing their arms and legs. I was shocked.

He was skeptical and unsure if anything could help me but recommended I fly up to Johns Hopkins to see Dr. David Hungerford, a giant in the orthopedics field. Oh, and I had to do it right away because he was within a month of his retirement.

What did this mean? Infarcts? Bone tissue death? How do they fix this? Can they fix this? I had so many questions. I was scared.

The travel was arduous—even grabbing groceries or turning a pancake on the stove was painful—but I hopped on a plane to Baltimore. It turned out I was the third to last patient Dr. Hungerford would see before he retired. What a pleasant surprise it was to meet him. He wasn't like any other doctor I had ever met. When he greeted me he asked if I wanted a coffee. We chatted about our lives for what seemed like forever and I remember thinking this was truly the first time I felt "heard" by a white coat. It was a lovely visit. He ran a battery of tests and the following day he diagnosed me with something he said he'd seen before only twice throughout his long career. I had osteonecrosis, the death of bone tissue due to lack of blood supply, in all four of my extremities.

The doctor who'd told Brendan years before that I'd be scarred for life following the complications I suffered due the retained placenta was right. Dr. Hungerford seconded what the rheumatologist had said, explaining that when I was hemorrhaging, my blood pooled to my vital organs—and I was lucky I hadn't lost my arms and legs. That loss of blood, combined with tachycardia and a dangerously low blood pressure, caused the bones to die.

The pain I'd been suffering through was very real and serious—the intraosseous pressure I experienced was something seen in bone cancer patients. OMG! And I'd been trying to muddle through without taking any pain meds, even Tylenol. I knew, and God knew as well, to persevere.

While this condition was deadly serious, Dr. Hungerford said it was mostly the metaphysis—the neck portion of a long bone—that was dead as well as parts of the epiphysis—the rounded ends of the long bones. Had it been mostly epiphysis that died, my prognosis would have been even worse. His interpretation was as follows:

"I believe that through the post-partum period, the patient developed microinfarcts in the metaphyseal regions of multiple long bones. This has produced intraosseous scarring and disruption of venous drainage of the long bones. Activity results in elevated intraosseous pressure elevation that causes the pain that the patient perceives and this limits her activity potential. Although I think it would be possible to provide this hypothesis with a series of "experiments" of sequential measuring of intraosseous pressure, this would be fairly complicated and I don't believe is necessary. The patient is significantly handicapped. Decompression is likely to be successful and could be carried out as a low-risk procedure that has a significant possibility that it would produce symptomatic relief. I am referring the patient to Dr. Carlos Lavernia for evaluation and consideration for implementing this recommendation."

The brutal truth was that 80 percent of osteonecrosis patients lose a joint. It just collapses. I knew there was a very real chance this could end up being my fate. There was no guarantee my epiphysis would not collapse as well. The odds were not in my favor. Most people have just one joint affected but I had four—in both arms and both legs. I was so frightened. Would I be able to even walk in a month? The pain was so overwhelming that I didn't know.

Once again I found myself without my health, not able to live a normal life—and now facing a huge decision when it came to available treatments. I returned home and immediately made many calls and exhausted all options. Basically, I had two choices. The standard treatment, core decompression, involved drilling into the area of the dead bone and inserting stem cells to stimulate new growth; if I chose this route I would be in a wheelchair on and off for two years. The second option was experimental, hyperbaric oxygen therapy, which involved breathing pure oxygen in a pressurized environment; if I chose this route I would have to lie in a hyperbaric chamber for four to five hours a day for months.

Diving For A Healthier Future

It was not a hard decision for us. I didn't want to be wheelchair-bound for two years. The rheumatologist I had seen put me in touch with a doctor in Jupiter, Dr. Cook, who fortunately was heading a hyperbaric oxygen therapy study. I was able to participate in a three-month study at the Jupiter Medical Center using its monoplace hyperbaric chamber, a clear glass tube that holds one patient. The schedule was grueling: three-hour "dives" for five days, then two days off, repeating until we reached twenty dives. Then I had two weeks off then before an MRI was taken to check for progress.

Now let me tell you a little about life in a mono hyperbaric chamber—at least back when I did it in 2011. Because the chamber was grounded and needed to be free of any flammables, I had to be grounded before each session. That meant having clean hair (no conditioner), not wearing makeup, nail polish, or even tampons, and putting on a special gown that almost felt like something to be worn in a prison. And if any of my vitals were off, I wasn't allowed in. As you might imagine, I couldn't bring anything into the chamber with me, like books or magazines. I was able to watch DVDs as I lay on the bed—and I must have gone through every one that was out at the time.

The chamber almost reminded me of those drawers you see in a morgue. Once I was ready, I was locked in and the air started pumping. I felt pressure in my ears as I descended into a dive—with the aim being to get pressurized oxygen into my platelets, which would then bring oxygen to the dead tissue to spur regrowth.

It was an exercise in faith for me, since it was absolutely terrifying being locked into a chamber and told an immediate exit is not possible. You can't get out for at least ten minutes so if you panic you're on your own. What was I going to do? Take valium for every dive? No. I chose to see it as an opportunity to practice anxiety coping skills. Not being a fan of claustrophobia, it was an exercise in calming my panic. I would sometimes feel my heart beating out of my chest—and I would just say "breathe—slow breath" and remind myself this was healing me.

This treatment was totally draining. I would wake up at 5 a.m. so I could get to the hospital by 6 a.m. and be in the chamber by 7 a.m. I remained inside until 10 a.m., was then monitored for thirty minutes, and usually was home by noon. When I was outside of the chamber almost all I would do is sleep, sleep, sleep. I admit I started to wonder whether it was healing me at all—but I took some solace in remembering what an old friend had told me: your body is healing when you're tired.

I did try to make the best of my situation. I brought donuts and bagels every week for my dive buddies, most of whom were in their nineties; they were tenacious and brought me courage. I was thirty-eight and each day I soldiered on. Both of my kids were in school by this time and I had a babysitter to help get them there. They came to see me in the chamber once but it scared them and I said never again. I carried on.

After three months there was no change in my MRI. I was understandably discouraged. The trial ended but the doctors presented me with the option to go on. I was listening to my body and just felt I should continue—so we pressed on.

At this point in my life, connecting inwardly allowed me to understand the need for reflection in quiet—and I had a lot of it. Every day in the glass tube I took time for prayer. I practiced harnessing clarity—tuning out the interference and noise of my wants, needs, and thoughts—to listen and just be. I asked questions in the stillness, such as is this healing me? Then I just sat with what came, listening to the cues that aren't vocal—tension, thoughts, fears—just letting them go by, through me, with me as the observer. I was taking note, paying attention to what I was allowing and not allowing into my mind, space, and heart.

Every day I dove I did this and some days were clearer than others. It didn't matter to me. I was tuning in. This was the infancy of finding God. Although I was practicing discernment minimally, it was a baby step to understanding something was there in me, with me, helping to navigate what was best for me. Over the first three months I connected within but felt I needed more.

Each time I would go back in I started to feel disappointment. Nothing had changed and it had been months. They were going to make me stop but I begged them not to. At four months, it was difficult to believe but I felt a small change; my arms felt a bit lighter, a bit less painful. I couldn't believe it. I still couldn't raise my arms over my head but I finally was encouraged—and we pressed on. At six months things really started to improve. We saw changes in my MRIs (see Figure 1)—the black and white infarcts on them were muting to gray—and I was able to start moving my body without crippling pain.

It was nothing short of a miracle. Pressurized oxygen gave me my arms and legs back. I was in shock for a short period of time. It actually worked. God guided me 100 percent through that.

As more months went by we kept seeing improvement and ultimately all four of my metaphyses were healing. Toward the end of the eleventh month of treatment—yes, I was in that chamber five days a week for nearly a year!—I was in the chamber and all of a sudden I didn't feel well. My worst nightmare came true in the tube. My eyes wouldn't stop moving side to side and I felt out of touch with reality. The doctors were called in immediately. Here I was experiencing an emergency, the one thing I feared in the tube, and no one could get to me for twelve minutes. Although at the time I didn't know what was going on, it turned out I was having an oxygen seizure. I'd never had a seizure in my life. I didn't know what I was feeling. The doctors felt that was about as much as I could take so the treatments stopped. It was to me a sign from God saying you are healed, there is no more need for this.

I continued to see benefits because with hyperbaric treatment the changes come weeks later. For example, what was being done at month three or four would be felt and seen at month five or six on an MRI. As you might imagine, I became a firm believer in hyperbaric oxygen therapy. It saved me.

What a whirlwind; I'd spent another year of my life in a hospital. I'd had to stop riding horses, stop volunteering, stop having a normal existence because I was spending the bulk of my time inside that chamber. Looking back, I realized there were warning signs that something was not right—I always had intermittent pain and most days the only way I could dismount a horse was to slowly slide off the saddle. I chose not to deal with any red flags because I just wanted to live my life.

It is very difficult in life to practice discernment—to tell the difference between your pain and symptoms and the healing process. Is this pain pathology? Is this pain from the wreckage of a toxin through my veins? You can and often will feel pain while you are on the mend.

I had gone to so many physicians who had come to so many various conclusions. I figured since I was able to tolerate the pain, I chose to live with it and move forward.

Goodbye To Florida

In 2010, Brendan's career in the NHL came to end after fifteen years. Because of all his job-related travel, he had never spent a full year in Florida. Plus, we usually spent summers at our cabin in Colorado or with family in Canada. As I was starting a new chapter after my experience with hyperbaric oxygen therapy, Brendan was also facing a big change: retirement.

You read a lot about professional athletes who have a hard time adjusting after their careers are finished but that was not the case for Brendan. He'd accomplished every major dream he'd had as an NHLer—playing 900 games over fifteen years, serving as a captain and a mentor to younger teammates, and competing in the Stanley Cup playoffs. He was offered coaching jobs when he announced his retirement but he turned them down; he was done with the professional sports lifestyle.

Brendan and I are very private but living the life of an NHL player is not a private existence. It is fast-moving, hectic, and full of interviews, meetings, and other commitments on off days. The idea of moving to complete solitude was super enticing for both of us. Our pendulum was about to swing completely to the other direction. With all the stress of my illnesses and his career it was much needed.

Brendan was psychologically ready to hang up his skates. He was into other things, like surfing and photography, so he wasn't lost when he left hockey. However, the year he retired he spent more time in Florida than ever and realized he couldn't handle the heat. He started searching for a new place for us and found a beautiful ranch in Montana. In 2012, we flew out there with the girls and made the decision as a family to relocate there.

Brendan and I needed quiet. He'd spent his whole adult life in the limelight, living a fast-paced life full of stress, so he needed downtime. I'd spent so many years being ill. We both wanted to reconnect with nature.

Montana brought a much slower pace of life, much needed for both of us. Our home was in the middle of a national forest. Our closest neighbor was four miles away. The nearest Starbucks was fifty miles away. The girls' school was a fifteen-mile drive each way. We didn't mind. At this time in our lives, reconnecting with nature and values was what was important to us. We nurtured the girls, spent time together, and slowed down.

#3 Witt's Its

- It's easy to be so thankful to be alive—and perhaps too fragile and breakable—that you don't journey inward.

- In the bottom of your heart, you usually know it is better to be aware what thoughts and feelings you give authority to.

- Pay attention to what you are allowing and what you are not allowing into your mind, space, and heart.

Chapter 4

Mind Games

My ongoing health issues did more than mess with my body—my mindset was deeply affected as well. I felt inadequate. Why couldn't I just be asymptomatic? It seemed there was always something wrong with me that I could barely make it through. I couldn't eat without some kind of side effect—and I'm not talking about bloating, belching, or having a stomachache; I'm talking riddled in pain, sometimes with blood (but nope, it wasn't Crohn's or IBS). I couldn't get out of a chair without experiencing pain. I was fatigued and weak. But I looked fine.

When you're ill, I think people expect you to look sickly. Externally I might have seemed "normal" but I was far from it. While I could function, I was often in pain and suffered from bowel issues, weight gain, and severe heartburn and indigestion that caused me to sleep poorly at a forty-five-degree angle.

Going from doctor to doctor was frustrating. They would want to give me extreme drugs when my body could not even tolerate Tylenol. I was convinced if I took them I would not survive. But I kept trying to find the cause for all my health woes even though all the tests I took didn't show anything was wrong. Everything looked great on a fluoroscopy, a urologist found only my magnesium was low, and a digestive specialist suggested I had celiac disease but wanted to do an endoscopy before making that definitive diagnosis.

After my previous experience with going under, I was dead set against it. I thought it would take me days to feel somewhat like myself. I insisted on being awake for the procedure, even though the doctor said he had never done an endoscopy on someone who wasn't sedated. He didn't know me.

It was not pleasant. And when I say that I'm being kind. A long tube with a camera on its end was snaked down my throat to my stomach. I retched—who wouldn't?—and the doctor said if I kept doing that he would have to put me under. I gritted my way through it, even when they took a biopsy from my stomach to study. I went inward, completely removed myself mentally from the situation. I stopped retching and the procedure went on.

The doctor told Brendan his idol had been Arnold Schwarzenegger but now it was his wife—me. Honestly, I didn't want to be tough. I just wanted to find out what was wrong with me and live life the way I wanted to.

The results were negative. I was told I was fine. Again. And remember this for later: no one ever suggested I get a full-body MRI.

Listening To Myself

While the many doctors I was seeing couldn't seem to get a handle on what was wrong with me, some people in my life had their own opinions. I remember being at a social get-together where an acquaintance told me her pastor said I was cursed but he could remove it. Another acquaintance told me during a phone call I must be an angel because God gave his toughest battles to his angels. And a third acquaintance told me all of this was my karma based on one or more previous lives. Wow! Really? Those were mind-blowing comments to me—how could anyone know that or think it? The sheer audacity! It was self-aggrandizing to the max. Honestly, to hear statements like these showed me more about them than possibly believing in any of what they were saying. What kind of an ego must you have to think you know all the secrets of the universe? You and your witchcraft believe you know the secrets of God, the afterlife, what happens to you before life and after death? You can guess but that's all it is. A guess.

I've come to realize something about those comments—they had nothing to do with me but everything to do with them. What was their motive? These were people's beliefs, not truths. No one except God knows the *why*. We are fed a lot of misinformation in life just because someone "believes"; a belief is a far cry from being a universal truth.

What were people trying to accomplish making statements like those? I remember asking the person who said I was paying for bad karma, "What is your intent in saying that to me? Saying I am condemned to a life of mental and physical anguish because of something that happened to me in past lives? You really believe this is true?" Her answer, shockingly, was yes, it was out of my control.

I kindly deferred and said, "You are not God. Your belief is just that, your belief, not mine. It doesn't make it truth. No one knows if past lives are real. Have you come back from death, actual death—complete with rigor mortis and being buried or cremated? No, no one except for Jesus, and a few in scriptures in the Bible has claimed to do this." My belief other than these statements being a product of a grandiose ego and deceptive advice is that when people say these types of things, they aren't meant to make you feel good. They are in a sense hurtful statements. Needless to say, those who made them were not in my inner circle.

People love to believe they have all the answers to the universe. It is everywhere, since the dawn of time—the charlatans, clairvoyants, all who claim to know more than most. In my experience with these people, I find the ones who claim to know it all know the least. Sometimes these people are driven by money; this is a billion-dollar industry. Ask them, what are tomorrow's lotto numbers? There's always a reason they don't know them. They need answers to inexplicable things—a child dying or something else horrid—and find solace in these platitudes. Certainly everyone is entitled to their own opinion but they are not entitled to make up their own truths. At least no one suggested someone was sticking pins in a voodoo doll featuring my likeness.

I mentioned before that I wasn't raised with having faith to pray for discernment. I was raised scientifically, to believe doctors were supposed to be brilliant and know *all* science. My insecurities and lack of confidence led me to question myself, question that little voice that kept saying something isn't right even when the "experts" claimed nothing was wrong.

I ultimately did have an epiphany, a lock and key moment when I knew I needed to follow the path I chose for myself. I began listening to what I felt was an inner guiding voice—my intuition, higher self, God? What was being told to me? I know something is wrong but I have no idea what. The message was coming through but the station was still staticky; I was hearing something but I wasn't paying as much attention to the voice as I should.

I say pay attention to your body—it gives you cues. I know God was telling me to listen to what He was telling me. Looking back, I would have persisted more. I let fear and lack of confidence prevail and continued to grin and bear it even though I *knew* and was being told daily "this isn't right." You don't have to go through the many illnesses that have plagued me to speak and communicate with God, i.e., your inner self. I began to feel this clarity more and more by calming external stimuli, turning off all distractions, and going to a place where I feel safe, quiet, and peaceful. You can too. Then pay attention to what is coming at you—thoughts that roll by. God speaks to you at your heart space.

It is a process to filter through being still—a capacity of observation and examination turned inwardly; a listening to yes this is right, this is what is best for you; an energy shift inward to truth. Your truth. God's truth.

Why do we not want to go inward? Going inward is frightening. Why else do people spend so much time avoiding it? Being alone with our thoughts is overwhelming for most of us. Our most intimate thoughts, fears, and vulnerabilities are what we discover when we go inward.

Do you not deserve to have peace in your life? Out of compassion for yourself, can you look inward and let go of the things that have brought you pain even when they're stuck? Beginning to love yourself is for most people a change in attitude, an evolution of love, loving yourself and others around you. Commit yourself to God, i.e., higher self, intuition, or a higher being, and devote time to your spiritual evolution. You deserve all the happiness this life can give you. Learn to sit with yourself and connect with your guide.

If there is good there is evil. Yes? I believe the devil—negative energy, yin/yang, black/white—is also around us. Those voices that fuel fear, that pull us away from God, are darkness. Who are you going to give authority to? The devil can be very convincing. When you are favored by God you are also favored by the devil, and I was battling demons.

Believe you are a child of God because you are. Let go of the guilt—the should've, could've, have to's you didn't do. God forgives you if you just ask him. Let those negative voices drown out and the light of God, the being you are meant to be, shine. It doesn't mean those voices aren't there; it just means you are not giving them authority. Let them be there. Don't react to them. And if you do, give yourself grace and let go.

I needed to listen to my inner voice—to do otherwise would bring fear in and cause me to wonder if the doctors really were right and everything was in my head. I knew better. I always knew better. But discerning through my doubt was the beginning of my awakening.

Where does that inner voice come from? Some say it's your higher self. As I noted before, I've come to believe that voice is God. I'm not a religious person but I am spiritual, and I found my faith from feeling completely alone in pain and realizing I needed some help. And remember it's never too late to realize that spirituality exists—there is more than just you.

You can never forget that you know you best—even if you are not confident in yourself. Also remember that when you're going through tough health challenges, there's no way you're not sometimes crumbled on the floor crying—but it's what you do afterward that matters. Plus you must be raw; share how hard things are instead of always saying, "I'm fine."

The mind and body connection is very deep so you must pay attention when something is wrong since your body speaks to your mind. You may not know exactly what your body is saying but you do know the direction.

Most importantly, don't think courage is the absence of fear—courage is being scared to death but finding the 1 percent in you to get up anyway. Plus, focus on having aha moments—connections with the great divine spirit that loves you and guides you. When you are connected to it, it is like a bullseye hitting the target.

Alternative Therapies

From the day my health issues started, I really thought Western medicine would cure me. And I kept giving doctor after doctor a chance to get to the bottom of what was happening to me. But slowly, perhaps too slowly, I opened up to the fact that Western medicine was not helping me.

I tried all the alternative therapies that were available to me in Montana and even flew to Seattle for some others. And I tried everything—including Myers 'cocktails (IV vitamin therapy), acupuncture, yoga, meditation, massage, and homeopathic doctors. I turned to Chinese medicine, figuring 5,000 years of healing couldn't be wrong, and found it was gentler on my body. I even did a sleep study because I found it hard to breathe at night.

All the trial and error was extremely draining on me. I still couldn't do something as simple as jump. What was going on with me? And why? I felt disabled. I was okay to function but not living the way I wanted to. If I sat for too long I shuffled when I got up to walk; I felt like an elderly person and I hadn't even celebrated my fortieth birthday.

I loved being active and found my purpose in working with animals, moving my body, and being productive. But I was unable to do any of those things. My body just wouldn't cooperate.

I never wanted anyone to feel sorry for me, especially when I thought of the families I was blessed to work with because of our assets and Brendan's high profile.

Witter's Hitters

Having money was new to me. From the start of our marriage, Brendan and I were on the same page—we couldn't just be consumers; we had to make a difference. So we founded Witter's Hitters in 1998 when he was a member of the Washington Capitals to allow seriously ill local kids to have an amazing experience at an NHL game.

Every month of the season, we rented a suite and invited kids who had cancer and other serious diseases like cystic fibrosis and muscular dystrophy, along with their families. These kids were gravely ill—some were hooked to IVs and had nurses with them. Thinking about my healthy girls, my heart went out to these suffering parents and kids.

Our goal was to provide them with a good memory and the game was just one part of it. Along with their VIP seats and access to treats like cotton candy and ice cream, the kids received #19 Witt youth replica jerseys and goodie bags. But the big surprise came after the game ended, when the kids got to meet the players and get their new jerseys signed.

Seeing the looks in the kids' eyes was priceless. I met so many amazing families over the twelve years we did the program. Two in particular stuck with me—one had two boys suffering from muscular dystrophy who were in wheelchairs and relied on vent tubes to breathe and the other was a family with five kids, three of whom had cystic fibrosis. One of those kids died a few days after attending a Witter's Hitters event, the last outing they had together, which was deeply meaningful for them all.

When I became ill, every time I started to pity myself I thought of all the brave kids I had the honor to meet. They had it far rougher than me and still had smiles on their faces. Kids are certainly resilient but I knew if they could persevere, so could I. "Get up, Sal!" That's what I would say to myself through the pain and tears.

The Value of Gratitude

As I moved through my health challenges I found it was extremely valuable to incorporate having gratitude into my daily life. It is so difficult when you are physically struggling to be grateful. I truly believe you can be grateful and depressed at the same time but you must find joy to move forward.

Despite everything I was going through, my life was blessed and I was thankful for it. Spending time praying and meditating was important to go inward—but not too much. It's a delicate balance. You don't want to begin ruminating. I remained mindful that I was raising children and wanted to be there for my husband. It was helpful to be living in Montana during this self-awakening since the slow pace of nature allowed me to focus on myself minus any static I experienced in other places.

Nature is God. It is the most healing place in the world. I truly believe that. If you can't be out in nature, envision it. Your breathing slows down, your shoulders drop, and stress starts to roll off of you. Try it.

From our very beginning of starting a family, Brendan and I always had a love for adventure and seeing the world. We enjoyed living in different areas of the world and were grateful to have the ability to do so. When life called us to Florida we jumped. And while we loved our time in Montana, it came to an end in 2016. We made the decision as a family to relocate to the San Diego area. It was an obvious choice, since our girls loved their time vacationing at marine biology camp there and Brendan loved to surf (none of that in Montana!), plus our oldest secured an internship at Scripps Oceanography in La Jolla.

Frankly, I was the least enthusiastic about our move but it ended up being the right thing for me because of what came next on my health journey.

#4 Witt's Its

- It's never too late to realize that spirituality exists—there is more than just you.

- The mind and body connection is very deep.

- You must pay attention when something is wrong since your body speaks to your mind.

- You may not know exactly what your body is saying but you do know the direction.

- What you hear is not intuition, a feeling, or a hunch; it is much bigger than that. It is larger than your mind. It is bigger than just you. And when you are connected to it, it is a bullseye hitting the target.

- Focus on having aha moments—connections with the great divine spirit that loves you and guides you.

Chapter 5

Horsing Around

We settled into life in the San Diego area, enjoying better weather and access to just about anything we desired. A trip to Starbucks was no longer a trek! My focus remained to live my best life even though I was still dealing with various health problems, from bowel issues that resulted in extreme pain to systematic weaknesses and fatigue. I had minimal strength and no stamina. I would quickly get exhausted but again every doctor I went to told me I was fine.

I found myself in a conundrum. Horses were my passion so I really wanted to ride again but truly at this time in my life I was not fit for it. This is an example of not tuning into what was best for me but what "I wanted." I felt an undeniable wish to pretend all was well and so we bought a young horse despite my frailty and limited abilities.

Sometimes in life we must ask ourselves some hard questions. What is my role in this? How did I contribute to this? Was purchasing a young horse a bright idea? Looking back, I knew better—so why did I do this? The answer to that last question was clear to me: I felt the need to prove to myself that I was fine. I could take on this task.

A young horse is not something to take on lightly. They require much more energy than a seasoned veteran. I was in denial, a mild denial. Haven't we all done this? We know if we go within and listen this is not the appropriate path for us. But in my headspace at that time, my thoughts, i.e., wants, took over decision-making. I had something to prove to myself.

Our horse was not a jumper. I knew dressage—the art of riding and training a horse in a manner that develops obedience, flexibility, and balance—was all my body could take; it would be less taxing than my previous exploits in show jumping. Even so, I could only ride for about ten minutes until I became absolutely spent.

Before I tell you what came next, let me be clear that I've probably ridden three or four hundred horses in my life and some were temperamental. I knew how to fall. Once I even had a horse roll over while I was riding it but I came out of the stirrups and landed unhurt on my feet.

Sadly, in the horse world there are many crooks—and almost always the horse pays for their maleficence. Many people drug horses so when you go try them out they're quiet and so level-headed. Nowadays there are drugs that go undetected, so even though we ran a blood test on this horse, nothing showed up. But the horse I tried out four times was not the same horse that arrived at my barn after we decided to make the purchase. Yes, it was physically the same young horse but it was unpredictable—rearing, bucking, acting chaotically like nothing I had ever seen before. My experience told me the horse we bought was not level-headed; he was volatile, and that was the last thing I needed at this time. But what did I do? I did not give heed to the warnings given to me.

A Bad Birthday

It was my birthday—April 20—and I was atop this unpredictable horse, sitting in a dressage saddle that supported the front and back of my legs. I was kind of stuck in there. The horse started acting up, rearing and bucking very near the edge of the dressage ring, and then he slipped, landing on his side.

I landed on my side too but my neck landed on the ring's wooden edge, about two feet off the ground—and the world went black. I was unconscious for seven minutes. When I came to, my vision was like a kaleidoscope—remember the tube you looked through as a kid and saw changing patterns when you rotated it? That's what I was seeing. For a moment I thought maybe I was gone. I could barely talk but managed to get out the words: call my husband. My poor husband.

Brendan raced to be at my side at the hospital, where I was in and out of consciousness. When I was awake I was vomiting, incoherent, and confused. And this was different than my previous health woes; it was the first time I had a brain injury. The brain—the headquarters for everything.

I had a Grade 3 concussion. If you look it up, you'll find the definition notes that symptoms from this type of high-grade, severe concussion can last for weeks before beginning to subside and permanent brain damage is a potential risk. I was certainly aware riding a horse comes with inherent risks, but this?

Because of the hard hit to my neck, I was also diagnosed with nystagmus—the crystals had been knocked out of my ears, severely affecting my equilibrium. I underwent a treatment that involved being seated in a rotating chair that was like something you'd see at NASA. The chair rotates crystals back in their place and to support your recovery you cannot do certain head movements for six weeks.

Immediately following my discharge from the hospital I was bedridden with insomnia, nausea, and vomiting; severe fatigue and dizziness; and an inability to think clearly on top of all my other health woes. I couldn't drive. I couldn't even understand a simple recipe. My daughter Aliana, who was in Hawaii, would be graduating from high school in six weeks. I was told I wouldn't be able to attend to see her big accomplishment—but applying mind over matter I was there.

I had to make my way back to normalcy very slowly. While doing even the most minor things, I would get an intense, overwhelming feeling that I needed to stop. It felt like someone was pulling at the back of my shirt, telling me, "stop, this is too much." And then nausea and vomiting would start. Fortunately, Brendan had been concussed—an all-too-common side effect of playing hockey—so he could relate to what I was going through. He was so brilliant in describing how what I was dealing with was all part of the process. He completely empathized and understood.

Of course I decided to put that horse out to pasture for the rest of his life. I deemed him unsafe and did not feel morally right selling him to someone given his volatile history.

Trusting Your Inner Guide

I write about this incident not to gain pity but to show you how easy it is to allow our psyches to make decisions that ultimately turn out for the worse. There is an inner battle between ego/self and letting go to God. The ego is like a caveman, very primal; it's survival brain. It's vanity, pride, and all me, me, me. It's easy for your ego to get in the way when there's a lack of clarity in deciphering the voice that guides you. I shared this event because I want to show you that so often in life we allow our pride to get in the way of the guidance God gives us, especially when it is an inner struggle between personal wants and what God wants. I wanted to prove something. I, the ego, my wants, overcame what deep down I knew wasn't the best for me. I had signs and did not listen to them. I remember before getting on this young horse one day, a loud, clear, distinct feeling of dread came over me. This was unusual, not the typical anxiety we all feel. Yet I pushed through it instead of pausing and listening.

What happens when you're able to silence and quiet your ego by praying or meditating is you no longer are taking all the pride and credit for all that happens to you but instead give the credit to where it is due. You let go and give it to Him. In return, you realize you are not alone; you acknowledge the things that happen to you are happening to you not out of coincidence or chaos but from divine intervention.

If I would have practiced prayer/meditation and discernment, I would have allowed those thoughts to just be—to let go of them and eventually give authority to my inner guide. I understand now that it can take you a while to pay attention, to be awake to hearing God—and all the outward chaos (TV, work, stress, etc.) are distractions to keep you away from listening to Him.

We are all human and we make mistakes. Buying that horse was a mistake—a costly one in more ways than one. It took me a full six months before I felt right again. And I was extremely wary about getting back on a horse for a long time, even though riding is one of favorite things to do. It was only more than six years after that 2017 incident that I got back in the saddle again for extremely short rides, maybe ten minutes. There's simply nothing like trail rides and enjoying nature from atop a horse but I know my limitations. I practice refined judgment to ensure I don't take on more than I can handle.

As I healed, I did start doing some things for me—in moderation—since my girls needed less "mothering" as high schoolers. I volunteered at the Los Angeles Zoo as a gorilla keeper and was a shark keeper at the Aquarium of the Pacific. I could work about three to four hours a day—and keeping busy was actually a painkiller for me. I didn't want to focus on my pain; I pushed through even if I was beyond tired because I knew otherwise I'd be just a bump on a log. That was not my style.

I had to learn how to deal with the new me since recovering from my bone disease and concussion, among other woes. I never felt quite "right." Looking back, I knew there had to be something else wrong with me. I was so tired all the time; I had hardly any stamina and what little I did was constantly draining away. It was like a Dracula-like demon was sucking out my energy.

#5 Witt's Its

- It may take you a while to pay attention, to be awake to hearing God.

- It's easy for your ego to get in the way when there's a lack of clarity in deciphering the voice that guides you.

- There is an inner battle between ego/self and letting go to God. The ego is like a caveman, very primal; it's survival brain. It's vanity, pride, and all me, me, me.

- What happens when you're able to silence and quiet your ego by praying or meditating is you no longer are taking all the pride and credit for all that happens to you but instead give the credit to where it is due. You let go and give it to Him.

- In return, you realize you are not alone, you acknowledge the things that happen to you are happening to you not out of coincidence or chaos but from divine intervention.

- You are loved and all the outward chaos (TV, work, stress, etc.) are distractions to keep you away from listening to Him.

Chapter 6

Losing Parts of Myself

It was now August 2018. I was able to do some of the things that were important to me. I was living life to the best of my capabilities! I wasn't fully back "on the horse," literally or figuratively, since I tired so easily but life is for the living, and dang it, I was living.

How I was able to walk without assistance boggled even my doctors. They were amazed that after having osteonecrosis in both of my arms and both of my legs that my ability to walk was not gone.

Something I'd never experienced, although I'm told it's fairly common, is a UTI. So when I felt something strange "down there," started having to pee all the time and it burned when I did, I went to urgent care. After basically being told to come back if it didn't get better, I went to my doctor, who diagnosed a UTI and gave me some antibiotics.

A little voice inside of me wanted more. I was listening more to my inner voice and did not want it to go silent. And I knew if I ignored it I would regret it. So I asked if we could do a scan. While acknowledging that wasn't a usual next step with a UTI, he said okay to an MRI. As the results came through, he looked at his intern and then at me—and suggested we do a CAT scan.

Uh oh. I could tell from the looks in their eyes that something wasn't right. Unfortunately, I'd seen looks like that all too frequently when it came to my health.

Eight Centimeters of Anguish

The scan revealed a tumor over eight centimeters long in my left kidney. Eight centimeters! For those of you who are metric system-challenged, that's slightly over three inches—gigantic in the world of kidney tumors, where anything over three centimeters is considered large.

I was stunned and I was angry. How could this happen? I was also in denial. I was dutiful about getting all my checkups, bloodwork, and preventive tests. I asked if it was possible that it was just a cyst and was told no, it's a hard mass, definitely a tumor. But it was unclear if I had cancer. More tests were needed to determine that.

Why me? No one in my family ever had something like this and I didn't drink or smoke—plus how had it gone undetected when I was constantly seeing doctors?

Wow! Brendan and I again thought back to the comment made by the doctor who warned us that I might be scarred for life. No one escapes septic shock unscathed. Having a tumor—a giant tumor at that—was a huge blow. All I could think about was it was cancerous and I was going to die.

When diagnosed with cancer or having a tumor, for me and I imagine for most people, we get completed wrapped up in our minds and lose the capacity to hear our inner self as clearly. I was consumed with anxiety. Do I have just a few weeks to live? Has it metastasized? So many questions I didn't have answers to. I was frankly livid, wondering what I could have possibly done to cause this.

It was a very difficult time. If there is anything I can say helped me through besides the love of my husband and family—which I am fortunate to have as I know not everyone does—it was to pull back the reins. Whoa! Stop and be mindful that this energy, this tidal wave of anxiety, is fear. Compartmentalizing this and being conscious of this helped me. I realized my mind became like the stock exchange ticker board and I just needed to let the digital show move through. There was much out of my control and all I could focus on was what I could control.

One of my first acts as someone with a tumor was doing what many people probably do when faced with any kind of medical symptom—I started googling. I must pause here to say I now know that was a bad idea and I really don't recommend it. There is so much bad information out there and it's extremely difficult to discern and filter. My suggestion would be to jot down questions for your doctor to find out what's internet BS and what's truth.

My searching led to heartbreak as I figured I probably had cancer but I knew I needed an actual diagnosis. That would come from a nephrologist, a doctor who specializes in diagnosing, treating, and managing acute and chronic kidney problems and diseases.

I called all the top-rated nephrologists in San Diego, only to learn no one had an appointment sooner than three months out. Knowing I had to be my own ally and I sure couldn't wait that long to learn my fate, I called every single day. I know they were fed up with me but to be honest I did not care. And sure enough, being persistent paid off when I got an appointment with the head of nephrology at UCSD for early September.

I was thankful and terrified at the same time. I wanted to learn the diagnosis but I was also dreading hearing it since I'd all but convinced myself that I had cancer. When I went to the appointment, the doctor took a look at the scan and said it most probably was cancer but another scan was needed, along with bloodwork, to determine if it was and if it had metastasized. It was almost too much to bear.

The Big C

Now this? Cancer. The Big C. After all I'd already been through, how much more could my body take? Cancer treatments have come a long way but that word is still scary, especially when it's being used to describe your condition. I don't believe anyone is ever ready to hear they have cancer. I wasn't.

So my fear came true. Now what? I looked at cancer the same way I looked at all my other traumas and illnesses—let's move forward and do what we have to do to get rid of it and move on. I also realized there can be vindication when you get a definitive diagnosis after not knowing what is wrong—even if that diagnosis is cancer.

The doctor said my tumor was too large to biopsy so I would need a left total nephrectomy—the removal of my left kidney. I figured I could live just fine with only one kidney as long as my kidney function was normal, and it was so far.

After hearing that stressful news we got another punch to the gut that my surgery wouldn't be scheduled—but we'd be on "will call." But thankfully it was just a couple days later when we got the call at night that my surgery would be the next day. I couldn't eat or drink anything from that point forward until after the surgery.

That fasting wouldn't have been an issue if my surgery had been in the morning but it wasn't. It wasn't even in the afternoon. It didn't start until a little after 8:30 p.m., by which time I was famished. Turns out I was the doctor's eighth surgery of the day!

Surgery and I are not friends; we've never gotten along. All the cocktails of drugs and chemicals affect me so deeply, resulting in sickness, nausea, and fatigue—all of it. I woke up from the anesthesia at about 11:30 p.m. in severe pain. Given my history I didn't want any narcotics but fortunately the medical staff was able to get my pain controlled with non-narcotics like Tramadol. The doctor gave me the good news that it didn't look like the cancer had spread but he would know more when the results from a biopsy came back. I spent two nights in the hospital and then went home to await the official word about what kind of cancer it was and whether it had spread beyond my left kidney.

Even though I was still in pain, I felt a lightening within me. I was weak but I had a sense of relief that I was not fighting anything anymore. I eventually learned that the kind of tumor I had typically grows at a rate of half a centimeter per year. That meant mine could have been growing for sixteen years (!!!) and its genesis was likely the complications I had from the retained placenta after my second daughter's birth. My significant hemorrhaging resulted in a lack of blood flowing throughout my body, causing abnormal cell production that was especially troublesome for my smallest organs, such as the kidneys, adrenal glands, and pituitary gland.

Can you imagine having a tumor growing inside you for sixteen years and not knowing it? It was mind-boggling to me. It also answered a lot of questions—why I struggled with indigestion, heartburn, fatigue, and weakness for so many years. I was harboring a tumor—that was why.

Ten days after the surgery I learned I had Stage 3 renal cell carcinoma. The margins were negative, which was good, and there were no necrosis factors, also good. It was the best news I could get but of course with cancer there's always the chance that it can come back. I learned that for the foreseeable future, every three months I would need to get a CAT scan, chest x-ray, and bloodwork to check for a reoccurrence.

Now what? The doctor told me to go home and live my life. No direction. No here's what you should do. No here are some names for alternative nutritional help and counseling. Nope, none of that. So while I was healing from surgery for six weeks I decided to read. I read until I couldn't read any more. I read how important diet and food were and felt the need to take control of my future by making some dietary changes.

I never drank alcohol or did drugs so I didn't need to change that but I stopped eating red meat along with white sugar, flour, and rice, and incorporated three cups of raw vegetables a day into my diet. Stage 3 renal cell carcinoma is advanced cancer. I had a serious chance of reoccurrence so I was determined to take control of what I could to better my odds.

Feeling Blue

I fell into a depression. I mean, how many near fatal and serious diseases could I be hit with? My seemingly endless medical woes had really taken a toll on my psyche and my body, with cancer being what pushed me to the brink. I had extreme trepidation about what would come next and I turned to acupuncture and yoga as well as seeking the counsel of psychologists on and off to try to calm my nerves and turn off the negative thoughts in my brain.

All of my suffering didn't add up to a good existence and I spent a lot of time being fearful. But my fear wasn't dying; my fear was there'd be no respite for me and I'd continue falling prey to more health woes. I was afraid to live—afraid of what might happen to me on any given day. Every morning I had to give myself a pep talk to motivate myself to even get out of bed.

I believe there is just a certain amount of trauma we can take, a threshold if you will before it is just too much. I had reached that. My will and mind were exhausted. I began to retreat inward, living in pain. Long suffering had finally taken its toll.

I was consumed. My body felt like it had taken as much as it could take. My mind matched that sentiment. I was plagued with dread on most days and an inability to see clearly. The life I knew I should be enjoying became arduous and I was filled with overwhelm. I became a recluse, stayed home. I was hit hard. I wouldn't say I had agoraphobia but again I was a bit afraid to live. What if I moved the wrong way and something else happened? I was really struggling, despite the fact that I'd always considered myself to be tough. I'd had a sink or swim childhood and that stayed with me throughout all my health issues. I even married a tough guy.

It was getting harder for me to cope with things. I found myself grasping for straws, holding on tight to anything I had control over because I didn't want to lose it. I would metaphorically beat myself up; why couldn't I just let go and move forward? I did practice gratitude, coming up with ten things to be thankful for as a way to work through the trauma—but it was tough.

I see it now that I was looking outward for comfort, for answers, for someone to tell me I was okay. I wanted a guarantee from life that I was going to be fine. This would, of course, not be happening, and therefore I was yearning for something that was unattainable. Therefore, I was continuing to suffer. There are no guarantees in life. I was grasping at straws around me hoping something would bring me assurance but of course nothing did. What I needed to do was go inward, working through the process that was always in me. And as I laid there wondering why I was so overwhelmed—I finally realized I had a choice.

I could continue to look at the darkness, the yin and yang, the sadness and the traumas I'd been through, and say it was just too much—protecting myself by staying home to live a boring existence of trepidation and fear. Or I could choose strength, light, love, and determination. True grit. Every day I would wake with what felt like a blanket of heaviness but I would not choose to let it engulf me. Slowly each and every day I made a choice. I would wake up and say no, you don't have to listen to this voice of darkness; you have been given life, now live.

I chose not to listen to the voices anymore that were telling me not to shower, not to go out of the house. Yes, they were there sometimes, screaming at me, but I wouldn't let the devil and his darkness prevail. I did not live through what I had so far to just sit around and be scared of more suffering and trauma. Despite my enormous anxiety and depression, I chose to change the gloom station, to push through. My body hurt and my mind was overwhelmed but I knew this would not last. After darkness there must be light. Half of every day we're without sun; does that mean we choose darkness over light? No, we make peace. Darkness prevailing is a choice. The battle of demons is real for all of us but remember there can be light in darkness.

I decided to volunteer at hospice, a place called Pacific House in San Diego, where I could bring joy with my licensed therapy dog to the sick and dying. I hoped this focus on happiness would lift the dark energy that had been around me and slowly it did.

I was paying attention to my mindfulness and started meditating and praying every day, looking inward to push through my challenges. I slowly began adding some kind of physical activity into my days—swimming, working out, and going on short hikes—taking care to understand my threshold. I felt a strength that hadn't been there before, probably because that tumor was gone.

I still had to deal with the trepidation that came before each follow-up scan but Brendan would encourage me to earn it, to envision seeing a positive result. And my first three-month scan was negative—as were all the other three-month scans over the first two years post-surgery. Then I graduated to having six-month scans, which so far have been negative too. While that is certainly good news, breaking through my fear was tough, especially at the start, as I was riddled with other potent emotions that were difficult to process: anxiety, anger, and even gratitude.

While I was taking baby steps to get back my life I was losing a lot of blood. On top of all the serious degenerative and potentially fatal diseases I'd overcome I also had bumps and bruises. My uterus was never the same after my second daughter was born. I would bleed so much that I became seriously anemic.

Lessons Learned

There are so many things I learned while I was dealing with cancer, starting with the fact that as I listened more and more to my station, things would get clearer and I would find better ways to navigate through anxiety. I also realized that while it was easy to let the fear of death consume me—feelings that were raw, deep, sad, angry, and dark—a healthier alternative was to surrender.

I needed to take control of what I could, letting go of all the rest and giving it to God. But I also chose a short time each day to devote to self-pity, anger, fear, and sadness—I gave it ten minutes—and then I devoted the rest of the day to love and living in the now. To clarify, when these difficult feelings would want to rear their heads, I acknowledged but did not dwell in them. I did not allow them to fester. These feelings can sit within all of us; it is what we do with them that makes a difference. I came to the realization that the fear was still in my head but I didn't have to react to it.

Finally, I discovered that when I felt stress and anxiety—my shoulders were all scrunched up and my jaw and hands were clenched—it was helpful to focus on breathing slowly to release my anxiety. Being mindful of the way our bodies hold trauma is important. The more I did it, the more natural it became—and ultimately I was able to let the crazy thoughts pass by like a breeze, like a wave in the ocean, realizing they were not permanent.

Major Surgery #2

The human body can only take so much. All the insults to my uterus finally took their toll. I started hemorrhaging again in mid-2019. Four times in four months I made trips to the ER. I was told I needed a blood transfusion if the hemorrhaging continued. I would go through a super tampon every thirty minutes for seven days. I could barely get up the following week even after taking iron pills.

Finally, I was told I'd need to have a hysterectomy. I had one ovary and one kidney and now I was going to be minus my uterus. I could almost make a mini-me from all my removed body parts! We were certainly no strangers to hospitals and surgeries but this knocked the wind out of us. Again, I would go under the knife for a major operation.

When I woke up from the surgery I immediately felt unwell and was running a fever. The doctors didn't know why I felt so bad—but I did. My body had finally said enough after going through so many inflammatory processes. The result was I did not have a quick recovery and again my life stalled.

#6 Witt's Its

- There can be vindication when you get a definitive diagnosis after not knowing what's wrong—even if that diagnosis is cancer.

- As you listen more and more to "your station," things will get clearer and you will find better ways to navigate through anxiety.

- It is easy to let fear of death consume you—feelings that are raw, deep, sad, angry, and dark—but a healthier alternative is to surrender.

- Take control of what you can and let go of the rest and give it to God.

- Choose a short time each day to devote to self-pity, anger, fear, and sadness—I gave it ten minutes—and devote the rest of the day to love and living in the now.

- Understand that the fear will still be in your head but you don't have to react to it.

- When you feel stress—your shoulders are all scrunched up and your jaw and hands are clenched—focus on breathing slowly to release the anxiety. The more you do this the more natural it will become—you'll ultimately let the crazy thoughts pass by like a breeze, like a wave in the ocean, realizing they are not permanent.

Chapter 7

Brain In Flames

I'd survived medical conditions that are often catastrophic, resulting in the loss of limbs, being relegated to a wheelchair, or even dying. I was minus a kidney, uterus, and ovary but I was still here. I was so grateful for Brendan's ongoing support—he has been my rock—and thankful that for the most part we'd been able to shield the worst of my health struggles from my daughters.

As I've already mentioned, it took me a long time to fully recover from my hysterectomy, my second major surgery in less than a year. I slowly got back into a routine but I never felt normal. Then in early 2021 I had a viral infection with symptoms like fever, body aches, and lethargy. Earlier in my life I'd had the flu, strep throat, and mono; this didn't feel like that. Was it COVID? I didn't know but it was awful. My pulse ox and vital signs were normal but I could barely peel myself off the couch for about three weeks.

Heading Toward Darkness

As I began to get back on my feet, I started to get awful migraines. I'd suffered through them before—severe, throbbing headaches caused by stress. I would get them usually once or twice a month, and rarely three times in a particularly bad month. I was familiar with pushing through the auras, enduring staticky vision like an old TV and squiggly lines moving across my visual field. But these were different.

First, I was getting two or three of them *every day*, and then they'd go away for a few days before returning. Second, the insides of my eyes were burning, like they were on fire. My vision started to go; I couldn't look at a computer screen without searing pain and I just felt unwell—sort of like a virus was sapping all the energy out of me.

I began deteriorating quickly after that. After starting to experience legendary dizziness—vertigo times a thousand—I went to neurologist who suggested maybe I had an ear infection. An ear infection?! I knew this was something far more serious than that.

I was not able to see well—and what I mean by that is an inability to track and gaze at objects; it wasn't blurry vision but more a lack of visual acuity in all facets. I was weak, experiencing pain in my neck, and I was barely able to walk. I also started sleeping poorly, waking up every hour and half in a panic and covered in sweat; I'd never in my life had an issue like this. Plus, my head would pound; I could feel my brain moving when I walked. Yes, I could actually feel my brain in my skull, something I had never felt before. What was happening?

I woke up one day and realized I was now stuck with a twenty-four-hour migraine aura. I had never experienced this—a scintillating scotoma all the time in my vision—and I was having trouble thinking straight. Those who get migraines know about that static on the television-looking crescent shape that develops at the beginning of a migraine and spreads throughout your field of vision; well I now had this in my vision even with eyes closed all the time.

My skin started to burn when anything touched it, even clothes. I encountered vertigo whenever I moved my head too quickly and had constant dizziness. I was appearing to lose aspects of memory and at one point I was so confused I asked one of my daughters when her birthday was because I could not remember it. I knew this was wrong; it wasn't as though I had no concept that this was something I should know—I knew this was something I should know and it therefore intimidated me. People who knew me and my ability to multi-task and retain information about my family and others knew this was very unlike me.

My thoughts began occurring in French, my native language. I was beginning to worry. Even with all my past health issues, I had never felt this before. I was scrambled inside my brain. When I would think about something words would come in French, in English, and mixed all around my mind. I was losing touch with reality. My neck began to become rigid—rigid like cement. It was like nothing I had ever experienced. It was impossible for me to turn my head to the left or right or up and down. And the pain was excruciating. I felt like I was losing touch with reality.

Changes in my symptoms occurred daily. After I woke up and tried to take a step, my eyes would start to shake. I couldn't keep a steady gaze at anything. I began to experience what is called oscillopsia, a vision problem in which still objects seem to jump, jiggle, or vibrate. Plus, if I would try to focus on something more than fifty feet away it was double—a car, a bird in the sky—everything was double. My whole world shook when I walked. My ears started ringing continuously. I was becoming more and more weak. The fatigue was eerily similar to the days I had septic shock. I experienced an overwhelming weariness and exhaustion that made walking ten feet difficult. My world was—again—falling apart.

In September, in the midst of all of this, Brendan and I took a long car ride. I remember telling him I was frightened about how weak I was; my symptoms were worsening and I would say, "Brendan, I feel like I am going to lose consciousness. I don't know how to explain it but I am continuously feeling this strange feeling like I am going to lose consciousness." I was so weak. As Brendan drove along, I looked down at my phone, my eyes saw double and faded out, and I did lose consciousness. I felt I was fainting but it wasn't like fainting at all. When I came to Brendan asked if I wanted to go to an ER. At first I just wanted to lay down. My world was turned upside down and nothing felt the same upon waking. I felt like I was underwater; my awareness was lowered to the point where I felt like I was going unconscious continuously and it was difficult for me to distinguish between dreaming and being awake. It was like being half conscious—that feeling right before you fall asleep—but I was awake.

We went to the ER, where they thought maybe I'd had a stroke but they couldn't find anything wrong. Of course not! They did MRIs and bloodwork; my sodium was dangerously low but they did nothing about it. They diagnosed me with a complex migraine and said to go home. This was during the COVID pandemic and that seemed to be everyone's concern at the hospital. So I went home, where I was bedridden. I started hallucinating—another symptom I'd never had before. I saw streaks when I moved my hands and colors where there were none. The pain was excruciating, my brain felt cracked open, my nerves exposed; it was one of the most painful times I've ever experienced.

At this point, my head and my neck were so swollen that the sides of my neck were touching my earlobes. I also couldn't handle any stimulus associated with living. Even my family talking to me would cause me to have a seizure. I couldn't think, move, or listen without pain. I needed help to walk to the bathroom, I lost the ability to swallow food properly—I could only swallow tiny infant-size bites of food—and my eyes felt ablaze as if paparazzi lights were on them all the time. There was no escape. Whether sound, sight, or touch were involved, I was in constant agony. I couldn't talk or a seizure would come on; I couldn't see or understand conversation. I was in pure darkness. Dr. Frank, who wrote the foreword to this book, came to visit me; he was at a loss for words, baffled at the situation as well.

I had never been in such isolation. Years back when I was in a coma it was black; there were no near-death experiences—it was as if I was asleep and woke up three days later. This was completely different—I was in horrific pain and every single minute I was in isolation, in darkness, removed from the world. I couldn't speak or be spoken to, I couldn't listen to anything and couldn't open my eyes because any light source brought agonizing pain.

My ability to be in this world was taken away. I laid there with my convoluted mind trying to decipher what was reality and what was not. When I would try to open my eyes my white kitchen walls were glowing in an amber hue. My eyes would burn so severely when I tried to open them for short seconds of time. I wasn't fully in this world. I was frightened and completely alone in darkness and deteriorating rapidly.

The pain kept increasing. There wasn't an end to it. In fact, it was getting harder to get through each day. I knew my mind and body couldn't take much more. I had nothing more. No reserves. No more energy. I experienced weakness and fatigue that felt like a one-hundred-pound weight was on me. It was over a month like this. I lost over thirty pounds and was now under one hundred pounds total. I laid on my couch with gun range headphones and a blinder—all day, every day.

The inability to move, speak, walk, talk, or eat well left me realizing I was near the end. I felt so alone. In this moment my faith in something greater than me wasn't secure. I felt something greater sometimes in my life but I wasn't fully in faith of God given my family's scientific background. After all the medical and life woes I had been through my heart was not open fully to faith in God. My heart was hardened. I felt the presence of God in nature—I would feel a greater spirit, the awe—but I wasn't sure what "it" was.

With that said, it did not seem authentic or moral for me to just start praying for God to save my life or to take my life so I wouldn't continue suffering. That notion didn't feel genuine. Oh, now you're going to believe in Him because you're dying, I thought. Up until that moment in my life I had never felt such loneliness. I was in a state unable to fully communicate yet when I tried I would be bombarded with pain. The isolation was heartbreakingly intense. It came to me to not ask for Him to take away all my suffering or save me but I asked in that horrid time if he would be merciful to me and for Him to be there with me so I did not die alone.

I said, "God, I am so alone, please be with me, please comfort me, a sinner. I ask for your mercy, please be with me so I do not die alone." I must have prayed it a hundred times. Looking back, I had no idea that this was eerily similar to the Jesus prayer. If I am meant to go I go. I didn't feel any epiphany, nothing had occurred. I was weak and frail and sat in this space quite some time, and after I don't know how long—maybe hours—I began feeling what can only be described as a sense of being enveloped by an overwhelming love, a pure, divine, unconditional love. My heart felt as strongly as if someone I loved more than life was holding me. My God, you are there.

I knew right then—although of course I didn't want to die—I knew either in death or if I lived I would be okay. I wasn't alone. I'd never been alone. My existence changed from that day forth. God had always been with me, and the suffering I was experiencing was bringing me finally closer to Him. It was an epiphany, as if in that moment, I realized all the suffering I had been through had to occur the exact way it did for me to come to this divine moment—that suffering was a divine gift from God. Yes, suffering is a gift from God. In that silence and tribulation was the loudest, clearest awareness of His existence. I understood he was always with me. With all the noise, literal and figurative removed from my life, his presence was profound.

One Step Forward, Many Steps Back

This was happening from September through December. I was bedridden, wearing headphones and a blindfold to cut myself off from all painful external stimuli. There was an acute process that lasted about thirty days and then months of torture followed. These months of isolation left me utterly alone—in my own self—with my whole body in pain. I was a prisoner of my mind and body.

Brendan and the kids took over every single aspect around the house. I had almost lost my ability to walk and talk, and any stimulus still caused me immense pain. Then I developed autonomic dysfunction—my nerves were unable to regulate bodily functions like heart rate, blood pressure, and sweating; It was uncontrollable, my resting heart rate was 140, far above the normal rate of sixty to one hundred, and I would sweat and have chills with no fever.

What was happening to me? I laid there in the hopes that it would go away. I had no confidence in any doctor after visiting the ER twice and seeing a neurologist, internist, and naturopath. It was the latter who came closest to getting the right diagnosis—an extremely rare condition.

I had never been in a state of so much pain. Everything hurt. When I tried to move, it hurt. When I tried to look at something, it hurt. When I tried to listen to someone, it hurt. My skin was on fire; taking a shower was done sitting down because of the weakness and dizziness and even putting on clothing resulted in needles of awful pain. Every factor of being alive was excruciating; I was utterly riddled with pain and didn't have much life force at all. I felt a deep force overwhelming me to not do anything, an inability to gain any strength at all. I was little more than skin and bones.

Was this MS? Was it Lou Gehrig's disease (ALS)? What was it? I didn't even feel alive. My whole existence had come to a halt. I'd faced health challenges before that were tough but nothing like this.

Thanksgiving came and of course I couldn't celebrate with my family. Brendan purchased a cooked turkey and he and our girls had the traditional meal but I couldn't eat or sit with them. I was laying on the couch wearing my headphones and blindfold, which I could only remove momentarily. My daughters thought it was just a matter of days; I was dying. So did I.

Since I could not communicate with the outside world, I would have conversations with God. Not that I would speak or have someone talk back to me but it was the only solace I felt. I learned during this time that His voice inside of us is very strong when all stimuli have been removed; I realized that voice is always there for all of us but because we are usually so distracted it is muted, it is difficult to distinguish. The conversations flowed. I would ask questions and would feel His presence through overwhelming sensations and feelings received. It began to be a practice of discernment through the months.

Christmas came and although there was minimal improvement I still couldn't take stimulus. Even watching the girls open their presents was overwhelming. This was not living. It was agony. But at some point I knew I needed to take off the headphones and blindfold; I couldn't succumb to the darkness.

After suffering like this for almost three months, and truly starting to think this was how my life would end, I finally decided to see a holistic doctor. I could barely make it to the car; I was in excruciating pain and Brendan had to help me walk.

This doctor suggested I might have post-viral encephalitis, which is usually treated in a hospital with mega doses of corticosteroids. Steroids? The doctor prescribed a low dose of hydrocortisone—ten milligrams for a week, almost like taking nothing at all, and it did nothing for me.

The doctor suggested IV vitamin therapy, and at the time I remember vividly thinking and feeling I was too weak for this. I was coerced by his pressure and hours after that IV therapy, I was in excruciating pain and peed what looked like blood. I went against my guide's voice. I returned to the ER and learned my spleen, gall bladder, and kidney were enlarged. The doctor basically said, "Whoops! Sometimes this happens," another medical flop, which was of no comfort to me at all. This was the last straw—and it sent me back to bed. The doctor added insult to injury and it threw me back another month.

Taking Baby Steps

This was not like any medical issue I'd had before. Usually there was an expected recovery time but not with this. Things progressed very slowly, way too slowly for my comfort.

Christmas passed and time went on. I noticed an ability to steadily be able to remove the blinders and headphones for a few minutes before needing them again. This was a tiny improvement. Finally, after three months I could tolerate literally living. My hallucinations went away and I was able to talk a little—but when I spoke pain would emanate from my neck and shoot from the top of my head through my whole body. I had many deficits. I continued to walk robotically due to numbness in my calves and legs and was dizzy for months. I struggled with swallowing and slowly retrained myself to swallow by going very slow with each bite and being conscious of the act of swallowing and over time it got better. I did not have tolerance for any stimulus for eight months and struggle with stimulus in general still to date. For over a year I only slept in thirty- to forty-five-minute cycles, waking as if there was a gorilla in the room covered in sweat for a year. This was the most difficult time in my life.

Throughout this dark time we were living north of San Diego near the Pacific Coast Highway, which served as a drag racing locale most nights. As you might imagine that loud noise was sheer agony for me, so in February 2022 we found a new home in the much quieter country. And when I say "we" I mean primarily Brendan. He also did all the packing, with an assist from our now-adult kids. I just had to get in the car and be driven to our new address.

Since I was still nowhere near to feeling like myself, I knew I had to get some help. It was hard to convince myself to go to another doctor because so many others had let me down. I chose to try a naturopath, and the first step of her diagnosis process was bloodwork, lots of it. A phlebotomist came to my home and took thirty vials of blood, which told an interesting tale.

It was a non-diagnosis of sorts. The only way to know for certain what I had would be to do a spinal tap, and I ultimately decided, after consulting with a doctor, that the risk was just not worth it.

Realizing I did want a more definitive answer as to what was wrong with me, in August I researched the best neurologist in the San Diego area but I wasn't able to get in to see him until the following February. As I looked forward to that appointment, I regained some normalcy in my life, even starting to cook again.

When I finally learned what made me suffer so much from that neurologist, I was stunned. It was encephalomeningitis, an inflammation of the brain and its surrounding protective membranes that resembles both meningitis and encephalitis. It is an unusual disease—one that often doesn't show up on an MRI or CAT scan—which explains the difficulty most doctors had in diagnosing it. My odds of survival were slim.

This extremely rare condition can be fatal if not treated promptly and many who have it are on steroids for many months to years if not the rest of their lives. I'd been on nothing. I survived it with absolutely nothing, not one pharmaceutical. I was fortunate to be alive. Actually, the neurologist stated it was unheard of for me to have survived this condition with no treatment whatsoever.

What caused this? I do know its genesis was a blood-brain barrier break because my anti-glial fibrillary acidic protein (GFAP) level was in the red.

What caused this? Many things, possibly cancer, a virus, the horse fall, only God knows. The type of encephalomeningitis was GFAP positive IGG. GFAP should not be in your blood serum. It was in mine. One year later, I returned to the neurologist and we rechecked my blood with a Mayo Clinic paraneoplastic panel and the IGG antibody was gone. Thank goodness.

A Changed Woman

As I write this I still don't have all my strength back but I can feel more of it returning every day. I know I am blessed in many ways because some people who suffer from brain inflammation like I did die or end up in a wheelchair. I am riddled with physical and mental shortcomings and every day my body is in pain—reminding me of what it has fought through to get here. My perspective is different. I earned all the pain and shortcomings. No one lives through this life without something they struggle with. We are given trials and tribulations to overcome in this life and some are more than others. Someone asked me if God was punishing me. What a strange question, I thought. What if it is the other way around? What if my heart was hardened and not open to God and He was desperately trying to open it all this time? One can guess.

I listen and am grateful. I listen to what I can and cannot do or undertake mentally. I honor His voice. When I hear guilt for not doing as much (should've, could've, would've), I remember not to give authority to that as that is programming.

Since we were children, we've taken in so much programming, like a computer, as authority. Our innocence and kindness when we were young allowed that programming in. We trusted it. But when you look within as an adult, that programming can be removed and your own shining light replaces it.

Don't buy all the garbage being sold to you—take this pill and it will cure you, do this every day and it will fix you, you need thirty minutes of cardio, you need this or that. Turn off Netflix. Remove as much of the noise—the internet, TV, radio—as you can to stop hearing what others think you should be doing, their thoughts, their theories, and their beliefs. When you let go of the guilt—the "shoulds"—and become aware of what programs you are accepting daily, what is being sold and exploited by others to capture your mind, your voice—your inner guide—becomes extremely loud. You're able to honor it and be guided by what is best for you.

Release the programming by letting go and forgiving. If you believe in God, ask for that forgiveness; if not, forgive yourself. You will be more liberated. Additionally, meditating and praying—tuning in to yourself—will allow for that clarity and the voice to be louder and able to drown out the garbage being told to you daily. When you remove the noise of the outside world, your station will be extremely loud and crystal clear. It just takes practice.

You do not need to be near death to hear your higher self, the great spirit, God, that voice inside. Remember that all great religions say to go within to be closer to God but it is certainly not necessary to even believe in God to hear your inner or higher voice. You need to go within either in nature or another space that is peaceful, safe, and quiet. I personally believe in God, wholeheartedly and unequivocally.

Please don't tell me you have no time for meditation and prayer. You have time to apply makeup every day. You have time to eat every day. You have time for things that are important to you. Make time. Pay attention to the energy in your body and the clenching, the tight areas that some call chakras I call tensing. Why is the energy not flowing through there? Why is it stuck? Why are you so uptight? The answer may not come right away but don't force it; it eventually will come, and if the why comes up short, pay attention and have the mindfulness to release it. The why will come to you later.

Finish your prayer and meditation sessions with gratitude, even when life is hard. It is extremely important to be thankful for what God has given you and what life has given you—three meals a day, a roof over your head, people who love you, a dog, whatever it may be. It is ultimately your choice to wallow in sorrow for what has happened to you or to rise and see what you were able to overcome with God's help. You handled it with grace and the best way you could and that is more than enough. You are here now, shining brighter then you were yesterday because of what you have overcome.

Of course it's human nature to want to heal ourselves and be guided to good health but if you are uncertain about what I say, ask yourself how many millions of dollars are spent on psychic readings, spiritual healers, horoscopes, etc. when God lies within you. God lies within all of us. We are his children. *They* don't want you to know this because then what would happen to their almighty dollar.

I can honestly say that what I went through was too much for a human to bear. I reached a breaking point where I had nothing, no more reserves. I did have new perspective; while I certainly did not want to die prematurely, I was comforted knowing that I am not alone. I am a totally different person—mentally, physically, and spiritually—than I was before.

#7 Witt's Its

- You do not need to be near death to hear your higher self, the great spirit, God, that voice inside. Remember that all great religions say to go within to be closer to God.

- When you remove the noise of the outside world—through meditation and prayer—your station will be extremely loud and crystal clear. It just takes practice.

- Remove as much of the noise—the internet, TV, radio—as you can to stop hearing what others think you should be doing, their thoughts, theories, and beliefs.

- It is not necessary to believe in God to hear your inner or higher voice. You need to go within either in nature or another space that is peaceful, safe, and quiet.

- Pay attention to the energy in your body and the clenching, the tight areas that some call chakras. Why is the energy not flowing through there? Why is it stuck? Why are you so uptight? The answer may not come right away but don't force it; it eventually will come.

- Finish your meditation and prayer sessions with gratitude, even when life is hard. It is extremely important to be thankful for what God has given you and what life has given you.

Chapter 8

My Spiritual Awakening

I've already touched on how important it was for me to connect with God during my darkest hours—when I lost the ability to communicate, to even think straight, and to tolerate any light or sound. But there is so much more to my journey toward embracing spirituality and acknowledging the presence of a higher power when I hit rock bottom.

And I must segue a bit to note that despite everything you've read about my life thus far, there's much more to me than my health woes. I consider myself lucky in many, many respects—I have two wonderful daughters; I'm married to the love of my life, someone who was a professional athlete, which allows us to live a comfortable lifestyle; and I have many passions, including a great love of animals that has played out in a number of volunteer pursuits.

This book notwithstanding, all the health challenges I've faced do not define me. They are roadblocks I had to overcome. But going through what I did has changed me forever.

With no purpose, no ability to function at all, and experiencing pain unlike anything I'd felt in my life, all I had was me. I went deep inside myself and many things went through my head, including what

I had been doing to try to control the outcome. I'd always tried to eat right, to exercise, to get enough sleep—so I should be fine. But no, despite my attempts at control, I got cancer and then I was suffering terribly, with no certainty I would ever be better.

I didn't realize it then but I'd been outwardly chasing a dragon, putting pressure on myself to live. And after illness after illness after illness, I just wanted to stop. Going through four major health issues in four years was just too much; it depleted me.

Nothing To Lean On

I've mentioned previously that I did not have a religious upbringing or much of a spiritual background. I also already mentioned my scientific upbringing—my family being made up of chemists and biologists. Remember it was my aunt who'd told me at a young age that after we die we just float around in blackness. What is a kid supposed to do with that?

When I was in my teens and through my early twenties, I was introduced to the concept of spirit through Native American beliefs. I went to pow wows with friends and learned that the Great Spirit was all around us. That resonated with me—it felt right.

I remember traveling from the suburbs of Chicago to visit friends who lived in the Wisconsin countryside, where the pace of everything slowed down. It was the pace of nature, which has its own drumbeat; it's not manmade. That is the pulse of the energy we are all connected to. It says in all the great books that nature was created by the divine one. This scant spirituality was all I had when it came to faith or a belief in something bigger than science.

Surrender And Accept

When I was completely lost, thinking I may perish, I prayed. I reached out to a higher power, not knowing how His presence might manifest. You've probably heard people say they see a burning bush or angels when they summon God but it wasn't like that for me. This was a feeling—a feeling that something bigger than me was with me. I wasn't alone. Nothing will ever take this away from me. The feeling mimicked the hug you would get as a child from a loving parent or dearly loved adult.

I experienced this feeling every time I prayed. I felt God's love; God's protection was all-encompassing around me. I was forced to go inward, relinquishing things like guilt and shame, and I learned to surrender to what I was trying to control.

The energy that was beyond me led me to this surrender and acceptance. And it wasn't like surrendering to my situation or accepting being in pain but simply wanting a different outcome.

This feeling of love around me while I prayed—along with my family, of course—gave me the will to live, to not give up, to keep trying and keep pushing. This concept of surrender changed my view of life. When you want something so dearly, it's often the case of trying to put a square peg in a round hole but when you surrender, when you relinquish control to a higher power, the result is a feeling of peace unlike anything you have ever experienced.

After everything I went through in those dark days, I can say I now believe in a higher power, God, wholeheartedly. But I see embracing God as just one part of my journey of healing. Your own journey will be unique based on what God means to you—whether it is higher self, intuition, or something else.

We are inundated with external stimuli telling us what to believe, what is good for us, every single day of our lives. This makes it very difficult to tune into our channel—almost purposefully. Pay attention to all that is bombarded your way that causes your divine gift from God to be muted. Once you pay attention, and it enters your consciousness, you'll be able to see what is affecting you. I recommend adding as much time in nature as you can, since I believe nature is divinity. In essence your channel is communication with the divine. It is essentially stopping the noise from the world around and paying attention to what God is trying to tell you, connecting with Him.

Ignore The Charlatans

After realizing how much power there is to looking within for strength rather than seeking external stimuli, an important question came to mind for me: Why do we give authority to thoughts we shouldn't? I'm convinced this kind of thinking—ceding control—holds us back to becoming the person we're supposed to be.

For example, let's say you did something wrong as a young person—something against your moral compass that caused guilt and shame. As you mature and become a more ethical and moral person, you realize the error of your ways. Instead of holding on to any guilt you may feel, choose to go inward by praying or meditating so you are guided to release that guilt. You can free yourself from it. Ask for forgiveness, and picture yourself giving forgiveness to someone who has wronged you. Letting go is the single greatest accomplishment you can do for self-healing.

There is so much we do not know about this world of ours—and whatever might lie beyond it. Yet there are those who believe they have all the answers. Unfortunately, these charlatans, these posers, often convince others they have special knowledge or power they couldn't possibly have. There are plenty of people willing to sell you a bill of goods built on nothing but their own imagination.

Have you ever met someone who says Mercury is in retrograde so this is why things are going wrong in your life? Or how about this is happening to you because of what you've done in your past lives—you have to pay for it in this life? I mentioned karma earlier in the context of being told something that happened to me in a past life was the root cause of all my health issues. I've also heard people use that term to try to explain the death of a child. Sorry, but that is crap. Who knows what karma is? If it even exists? Don't buy into the concept of asking yourself what you did to deserve something.

Despite operating on no more than a "wing and a prayer," so many people want to tell us what they cannot possibly know. Who do these people think they are? And why are we giving them so much authority by assuming they know more than we do? They don't—and it's time we stop giving them this much power and giving away the God-given inner power bestowed to us by birth.

We don't know what happens after we die since no one's gone to heaven and come back with a report on the secrets of the afterlife and meaning of life. Dying on an operating table is not the same as being in rigor mortis for a week and rising from the dead; no one has done that so all these statements about life after death, karma, etc. are just theories; there's only one story of rising from the dead and that is Jesus Christ and he is God.

This brings to mind a story I read about the famous escape artist, Harry Houdini, who died in 1926. He was able to debunk mediums and prove most of them were frauds after promising his wife, Bess, that if it was possible to communicate with the dead he would come back to her—and he gave her a code to help prove it. After ten years with no success working with so-called experts, Bess stopped trying to contact him, saying, "Ten years is long enough to wait for any man."

I also have an example a little closer to home. I recall sharing an interesting dream I'd had with a friend—I was flying above this different world; it was a riveting dream. He says to me, you are experiencing the parallel universe your soul is in. I asked him how he knew this, who told him this, and he quips *they* did—that's what all the existential experts say. "What?"

We certainly have choices in life, which makes it amazing. You can choose to believe that we have special God-like powers to see into the future or past—or you can acknowledge this as just another unproven theory. The point to being mindful of what you accept as gospel is if you believe in these suppositions, you divert further from your inner guide.

When you buy into these suspicions, i.e., aliens guiding our actions, special God-like powers, stars, horoscopes, quantum healing, etc., you begin to look outward for answers about what is beneficial and guiding you. This, I believe, is counterintuitive to our God-given voice, intuition, and channel. When you do this you listen less and less to your channel and more to outbound and external stimuli.

You relinquish your inner guide to your own belief systems when you are convinced by programming externally, whether it's something you read, something someone told you, or something that made you fearful that ultimately sends you off searching for answers that are literally within you—or right in front of you. As an example, have you ever watched a program, been visiting with friends, or attended a conference where everyone shares with you the newest, latest supplement, patch, or bracelet—and says it will heal everything? You get super excited for a brief moment, and then what happens? Your inner voice says hmmm. Listening to God's word, your higher self, or your intuition is your consciousness tuning into that hmmm.

There are people who will tell you they have godlike powers, or you are your own God. Tell me, when is the last time you levitated?

Have you parted the seas? Have you healed the sick and yourself from all disease? Have you done what Jesus has done? No.

When we are at a crossroad in our lives, facing a health crisis, or are uncertain on what direction to take, if we are guided by the stars or whatnot, how are we supposed to hear our own voice? This is usually how regret happens, not doing what God was telling us to do. This is why it is so important if you want to tune in to Him to pay attention to what bill of goods you believe.

External sources are not the only way we are drowning out our own channel; it also happens when we go through stress, rumination, pain, and difficult emotional times in our lives—basically anytime we are forced into a state of being in our minds. In our ego, that is the voice of fear, of what ifs, which comes from the energy of the mind.

There is often conflict between this voice and your channel. When praying or meditating, pay mindful attention to this voice as an observer. Let it flow through. Question it. What if *that* doesn't happen or whatever the polar opposite of what the fear is? What then? Question the negative, question the dire outcome you are trapping in your mind space.

As you hone this process it quiets the mind. You begin to realize you can give authority to positive, more constructive thoughts. This in turn paves the way for your channel to come in crystal clear with what is best for you during this difficult time. This lies in your heart, your chest space. Whenever God speaks, intuition shines—it comes in the form of a release of a bullseye of energy in this space. You feel it without question.

I'm convinced we all have the power to go inward—without the aid of charlatans, crystals, or any other external support. I do believe some people have an innate ability to tune in quicker and stronger than others but that is a far cry from knowing the lottery numbers. And when I speak of charlatans, I don't just mean psychics or mediums—I'm referring to anyone who believes they know the divine laws of the universe. We simply don't.

As I struggled with my health, I wanted the will to let go of the things that brought me pain. I found that strength within myself during what I call my spiritual evolution, a newfound devotion to God. I believe everyone is capable of this.

Moving Forward

This change in me did not happen overnight. It took a lot of time to get to where I am today—along with lots of crying, anger, and new feelings. Now I am someone who is constantly surrendering—and has thus eliminated the pressure I previously felt about doing what's right. I realize now I was struggling inside, not giving myself compassion or attending to my needs.

Surrendering was like taking off a heavy coat—giving me strength to enjoy the moment and accept where I am. I am a firm believer that liberation comes when you let go of trying to control your life. Surrendering to what is has given me peace, calming my inner turmoil. It is in essence God's will, not mine, surrender to this.

I've realized it's so important to pay attention to the messages we accept daily—the programming telling us that we must have this car, or this lip filler, or whatever; the "Egogram" stories we read—always perfect; even the things touted by experts as being good for us. Buying into all this makes us not authentically who we are.

As I said before, like a computer, we're driven by the "programs" we put into ourselves. But we can't lose sight of the fact that we are the computer—we are not all the programs and the programming. When some of these programs become exploitative, our inner guide—God, light, and love—become more muted.

And what if that programming isn't the truth? For example, when I mentioned to a highly educated friend that I'd read an article about a benefit of taking Vitamin C, he quickly noted he could show me three other articles saying that's not the case. Anything—any data, any science paper—can be skewed toward what is being sold. A new pill? The science says it works and twelve documents say it kills you.

The supposed science is constantly changing. The narrative, the goalposts, they're always moving. Observe what your body is telling you after you eat something instead of paying dutiful attention to what the television is telling you to eat. We all know if you eat a plate of bacon every day of your life and you eat ice cream daily you will get fat and suffer from heart disease; we don't need the television to tell us that. You will see what happens if you eat like that—you will become lethargic and heavy and have difficulty with daily chores; your body will be talking to you. Your job is to pay mindful attention to the ways it communicates with you.

Remember when eggs were supposedly really bad for you? And then they were good? *They* don't know! So I say if you like eggs, eat eggs. Do what feels right to you. Certainly take care of your health—watch your blood markers—but care for your body because you love it, not because you're fearful of getting sick.

The overarching message is to stop going outward when you should be going inward. For me, that means praying and meditating on a daily basis and leading a life that's less bound to resisting the positives and accepting what is. This process has taken decades for me to hone it in through tribulations—fine tuning it to share with you. I was not one of the lucky ones who was in tune with their channel from a young age but now I know it comes through my heart space.

I was a slow learner when it came to realizing that the outward forces did not always "know best" for me so I allowed those voices to supersede my inner guide's voice. That voice was always there, staticky perhaps but within me all along, and something else was alongside it: my will to live. That is the focus of the next chapter.

#8 Witt's Its

- Nature is divinity—add as much of it in your life as you can.
- We are inundated with external stimuli telling us what to believe, what is good for us, every single day of our lives. This makes it very difficult to tune into our channel—almost purposefully.
- Pay attention to all that is bombarded your way that causes your divine gift from God to be muted. Once you pay attention, and it enters your consciousness, you'll be able to see what is affecting you.
- It is in our human nature to want to heal ourselves—we want to find something or someone to heal us and there are some things that do heal us—but pay attention to the charlatans.
- During difficult times in your life, your channel has difficulty tuning in. During prayer and meditation, pay attention to the voices of the mind that are not your channel since your channel comes in through your heart space.

Chapter 9

The Will To Live

After going through so many life-threatening illnesses, I simply cannot write this book without discussing how important the will to live is—the will to fight, the will to survive when you're in a fight for your life. I think it's fair to say I am not discussing the philosophical aspects of it—believing in divine intervention; when it is your time it is your time. I'm not going to profess I have discovered answers to questions that have befuddled people for eons.

My message in this chapter is simple but critical: it is important to fight like hell. And it is both a physical and mental fight.

As I noted in chapter 2, when I was falling into my coma, the deep sleep feeling that came over me was beyond anything I had ever felt in my life. It was the most encompassing, engrossing, heavy, toxic succubus. It was an absolute drive toward unconsciousness. I felt like a sumo wrestler was laying on top of me, an inescapable weight that would not allow me to even move my arms and legs.

I was dropping into an abyss. I knew at that moment in my life, I was at a crossroad. I could succumb to the sleep, the most peaceful, deepest, profound sleep I had ever fallen into, or I could establish a fight in my body. I remember telling myself, Salima, don't succumb to this, do not succumb to it. Even though I was falling in and out of consciousness, I had established the will—the will to live.

When Brendan arrived at the hospital, he was told I might not awake from the coma. I might die. But I woke up. I woke up—but with so many deficits. I couldn't walk. I couldn't hear very well; I liken it to wearing a fishbowl around my head like an astronaut—that's what sound sounded like to me. I was so weak, and the fight had just begun.

The will to live is painful. I chose motivation instead of apathy. That is not to say that within that fight there isn't sadness, anxiety, depression, or anger—there is all of it—but inside of you there is hope, there is motivation, there is a never say die attitude.

I faced being restricted to a wheelchair for the rest of my life. I faced raging sepsis. I faced cancer. I faced a brain injury that left me unable to speak. All of these have two common denominators: the greater voice inside of us that guides us through making decisions that are best for us and the absolute will to make that voice come to fruition.

Surgeries, illnesses, infections, cancers, tumors—you name it, I've had it. I personally believe when our time comes, it comes—but not without a fight. I cannot stress the importance of perseverance.

Fight for your life—you have a chance when you hang on to the will to live.

When we are faced with life-threatening illnesses or circumstances (accidents, trauma), we do have a choice. In our weakest moments, when we feel the most vulnerable, we can regain our power. How? Hope. Nobody can take that away from you. Not a doctor, not a diagnosis, nothing. With hope, we are able to prove the unexplainable, the miraculous healing that occurs.

This is not to say the people who have died from their illnesses did not fight; do not mistake my words. Those people lived a longer life than if they wouldn't have fought at all. Not only have I experienced this time and time again in my life, I've witnessed it as well. When I volunteered at the hospice I saw it for myself. The people who had apathy, indifference, they would go a lot faster than the people who still found joy, who still found fight, who still found a reason to be. I also witnessed when people knew it was their time and they found solace in letting go to God. They were ready, at great peace, and it was their time to let go.

I've also seen this with animals. When I've been healthy enough, I've worked with animals of all types—including primates, raptors, and lesser cats—and when they are actually given a chance to die, naturally, not by euthanasia, I've seen time and time again that they move to a quiet spot, pull away from society into a deep corner, and die. They stop eating, they stop drinking, and they stop socializing; they are ready for death. It is the same with human beings.

Why do so many people suffering from advanced stage cancer pass right after a special event like Thanksgiving, Christmas, or their birthday? There are numerous studies about this phenomenon; it's as if they say, "I made it to the special event. Now I am ready to go."

I've had many people tell me I'm just so tired, I'm so depressed. I don't feel much will. I do have an answer for that. The will to live is not the absence of negative emotions. It is not the absence of fear or anger or sadness. Many books will say people who have a strong will to live are driven by positive emotions. Poppycock! Yes, they have hope but make no mistake—when you are riddled in pain, fearful, and have very little emotional and physical strength, you may be confounded by difficult emotions but it is hope intertwined and encompassed within these emotions that is the driving mechanism.

People often ask me if had dark thoughts. The answer is yes. They do try to come in. And sometimes they force themselves in during the darkest of times. It is in those moments—at that crossroad—that you realize you have a choice: you can succumb to those feelings or you can pick yourself up from the floor and push through to get to the other side.

You don't know what the next day will bring you but I implore you to rise above when everything looks bleak. I believe it is one of the hardest things you can do in life. Two years ago, I was told by a neurologist that I would have severe mental deficits from encephalitis for the rest of my life. I was told by esteemed doctors at Johns Hopkins that my fate would be a wheelchair.

Of course there are issues I deal with physically and mentally daily after all I have been through. A warrior does not come out of war unscathed. But if I would have listened to what the neurologist said or what the bone doctor said, I wouldn't be where I am today.

I've been given life. It is my duty to embrace this gift. We've all been there. Losing a loved one, heartbreak, depression, whatever it may be, we rise above. Why? I have no family, someone will say; I have no reason to live, someone will say. But you do—you were given a gift and it's called life. You treasure it, you fight for it, you hold it dear.

My body and my mind have been through legendary battles—battles that have exhausted my mind and depleted my body. You have to replenish it with rest, love, laughter, less stress, fluids, and the fuel you put in your mouth.

Going through such serious health challenges caused me to take a long look at what I was putting into my body. Our bodies speak to us or in my case scream. I always considered myself to be a healthy eater but now I pay strict attention to everything I consume because I am a firm believer in the healing power of food. Obviously food in itself will not be the end all healer of all healings but it is I believe the foundation to begin to heal. I talk more about that in the next chapter.

#9 Witt's Its

- Fight for your life—you have a chance when you hang on to the will to live.

- You will have dark thoughts when you are very ill; that is normal. But you must make the choice to push through to get to the other side.

Chapter 10

You Are What You Eat

The ability to have the physical strength to go inward is partly if not wholly fed and driven by what we put in and on our bodies. That means food, creams, shampoos, perfumes, and more—everything matters. It is important to give your body the chance, the medicine it needs to replenish what it has lost—and I'm not talking about prescriptions or supplements. Give yourself a chance to heal through your daily intake of what you put in your body.

You've probably heard it said that some people eat to live while others live to eat. I was definitely in the latter group. Many, many years ago, I did experience negative symptoms from foods that did not agree with me but that did not stop me from being a foodie. I loved food, and I could eat my favorite—pizza—morning, noon, and night.

But that was *then*.

My diet today is fairly restrictive—actually quite restrictive is a better way to describe it—but it took me a long time to really listen to my body and pay attention to what it was telling me. Pizza and many other things I loved to eat are now a thing of the past. It's heartbreaking on the one hand but life-affirming on the other. And the journey was not fast or easy. But I do agree with the popular phrase, "Let food be thy medicine and medicine be thy food."

I believe food is one of the most basic and fundamental healing modalities we have. It can kill us, it can injure us, and it can nurture us.

Back To The Beginning

On top of all the major medical woes I've documented, I suffered from IBS, asthma, allergies, and hormone issues from a very young age. As far as I can remember I had stomach problems; I recall being scared I would poop myself in class. They called what I had spastic colon back then.

I grew up poor, so we ate what I would call appropriately priced food. I subsisted on a lot of Chef Boyardee and ramen, and I remember often eating mustard toast and ketchup on rice. McDonald's was a huge treat for us.

When I got married in my mid-twenties, I became more aware of the value of a healthy diet and started eating organic food but I ate everything: white sugar, wheat, and other "organic" things I would later discover were toxic to my system. I frequently had stomach pains and cramps and sometimes bled from my bowel—something I was told was a symptom of IBS.

Anyone who has suffered from a bowel issue like IBS knows it can be debilitating. I was so frustrated; so many foods bothered me. I would either be in severe pain from spasms and cramps or bloating or I couldn't go to the bathroom at all or I went too often. When I sat in prayer, it came to me.

I had spent most of my life listening to what the doctors told me. I had paid more attention to what they were saying then to my inner guide. They would say just take more fiber and you'll be just fine or give me a generic list of foods not to eat, which didn't help at all. I questioned what was happening, slowly peeling layers. The answers came to me; my body was screaming at me—I just needed to listen.

The doctors tell you this is acceptable. This is just the way it is; you're just this way. I call BS! Is that what they want you to believe? I remember in my twenties going to Georgetown Hospital and them telling me, yes, this is just IBS. Here are some medications to calm your intestines. You just have nervous bowel issues. What? Are they getting payment for the pill they are trying to give you? They will tell you to read books but the doctors who are selling ways to heal your IBS are also selling supplements and treatments—the opposite of integrity if you ask me. If the only way I'm going to get better is by taking your supplements or pills I think I will pass.

I recommend you be a skeptic and ask lots of questions if your doctor suggests supplements. Is it good for you? Or is it good for them? Supplements are known to have toxic levels of arsenic and other poisons in them. They are minimally regulated.

In my thirties, after a couple of incidences of seeing blood drops after going to the bathroom, I went through myriad tests—many colonoscopies, a CT scan, and plenty of bloodwork. I also had a celiac biopsy and blood test done and was tested for the protein found in wheat—and everything came back negative. Even as I heard the test results I knew something was wrong. But I was not yet at the point of trusting myself to listen to God and body to be able to act accordingly even when doctors were telling me nothing was wrong.

Now I know how important it is to listen to your inner voice when you are experiencing symptoms that seem to be related to the food you are eating. I listened to my doctors instead of my inner voice (and my body screaming at me) for so long—blindly obeying—until I finally wised up.

Eat For Health

After I had cancer, I was told to go live my life, literally. When I asked the doctor if there was anything I could do to up the odds of it not coming back, I got a quick no—go live your life. While I fully intended to do that I had come to the conclusion I had to figure out a way to help myself gain better health. I understood food is a huge contributor to our well-being; it can cause maladies but it can also cause wellness. I wanted the latter. If eating the wrong things could cause diabetes, gout, and high cholesterol then surely eating the right things could reverse it. I was determined to learn what I could eat for better health and to increase my odds of staying healthy.

I watched a TED talk by Dr. William Li, who I later got to know, the author of *Eat to Beat Disease*. What I learned from him was the foundation for me to start my journey of eating for better health. Right away, while I was still recuperating from cancer surgery, I started adding more raw food to my diet, including a green shake I drank twice a day with ingredients like raw broccoli, raw collard greens, raw kale, raw beets, raw bok choy, and one piece of fruit. Sound repulsive? It was.

I cut out white sugar, rice, and red meat from my diet. I continued eating whole grains though, since they were supposed to be "good"—but I was still having stomach and bowel woes. Finally, a doctor suggested perhaps my issues had to do with grains, so I had an anti-gliadin test done at a boutique lab and my numbers were through the roof. That in and of itself made no sense because the protein gliadin is present in wheat and therefore the initial tests I had should have come back positive. Regardless, since nothing else had worked I eliminated all grains.

Even though modern medicine tests said I could tolerate wheat, my body could not tolerate any grains at all. Is it the glyphosates? I was eating organic grains and still having problems. And two things immediately made sense to me: 1) my brain and bowel issues were intertwined and 2) I wasn't completely healed from my last illness. Actually, I knew the latter was true before this, since a year after my diagnosis the aftereffects were still with me, including numbness and tingling in my legs, flashing lights, double vision, and parosmia—things smelling weird. And the insult to my brain also left me with tremendous bowel pain.

The mind and body are connected. The brain and gut are connected. If you are suffering from any neurological disorder, any autoimmune disorder, or any illness that involves any of the above it is imperative that you look at your diet. I spent countless hours researching to learn that grains and dairy are toxic to the neurologically and autoimmune injured. It's important to be aware that healing from a life-threatening illness is multifaceted—and food is the building block, the most foundational structure of your health.

With painkillers never being an option for me because I was so sensitive to them—if I took two Motrin I would be in even more pain—what could I do? I radically changed my diet.

Detoxing

In addition to not eating grains of any kind—rice, corn, oats, bran, etc.—I stopped eating white sugar, beans, soy, and dairy. My diet consisted primarily of chicken or fish and root and leafy vegetables. The biggest bummer for me is not being able to eat cheese; I do have some French in me! Although recently I have incorporated sheep cheese and raw milk, after reading these types of cheese and milk do not trigger autoimmune issues. So far so good.

While there was some sadness at having more stuff taken away from me, that was coupled with relief that there was something I could do to support my ongoing health. But the first month after I started this radical diet I felt awful. It was like I had a one-hundred-pound weight on my chest again. I felt ill, flu-like almost. What had I done? I realized I was detoxing—and I did not know that would make me feel so awful. When I gave it some thought, for almost fifty years I had been eating grains pretty much every day of my life. I had truly not ever gone without. I was going through a difficult detox. I reconciled with this and moved forward. Slowly I started seeing the results I was looking for. Initially it was small victories, periodic pain that had lessened in degree, more regular bowel movements, a bit more energy. It took time—nothing came immediately. I noticed after six months I rarely had bowel pain, I was clear-headed, and I had much more energy.

Oh, in case you haven't already figured out that I have the greatest husband in the world, let me tell you that Brendan follows the same diet I do. "Let me do it with you," he said. I will say if my "don'ts" included chocolate it might be another story!

As I write this, it's been more than two years since I totally changed what I put in my body. I have been absolutely strict about my diet—no cheating whatsoever at first. I have incorporated red meat back sporadically and there has not been any trouble digesting it. But I did not do this until I was two full years on this rigid diet. I wanted my gut to heal and that meant no cheating. But since life is meant to be lived, I'm hoping sometime in the future I can enjoy a little cow cheese, no more than every couple months. I really miss many of things I can no longer eat but I certainly don't miss the woes that resulted from putting the wrong things in my body.

I also learned as I was educating myself about the healthiest diet for me that I have an intolerance to FODMAP—short-chain carbohydrates that are poorly absorbed in the small intestine and prone to absorb water and ferment in the colon. That includes sugars, onion, and garlic. Limiting those truly helped but I'm not going to tell you it was easy. It was a difficult time. Truly, I felt I had gone through so much and now I'm basically eating like a bird. I allowed myself self-pity for a minute then that was it. I was alive, I was able to live, and God willing that was what I was going to do.

I was afflicted with so many ailments that it was difficult to discern what I was eating that might unwittingly be causing me to suffer. As I was praying, some of these answers would come to me, although healthy eating, I've learned, changes through the years. I have needed to adapt to nutrients I lacked and nutrient abundances and make alterations, which is why I am a big advocate in checking nutrient levels. I drank or shall I say ate those green shakes on a daily basis for over five years until I learned I was lacking in some essential vitamins and minerals. I thought how could that be—well let me explain. I was eating a cup full of green leafy veggies twice a day for years, then it hit me. I woke up with peripheral neuropathy and a severe weakness in both legs. Luckily, I had a brilliant naturopath doctor who checked all my vitamins and nutrients, and lo and behold I had a severe copper deficiency. My naturopath and I were stumped; I ate so well and all my other levels were good. I thought how in the world did this happen, and after much prayer and inward reflection it came to me. Oxalates deplete minerals, and I was eating a ton of oxalates. So I slowly started to cut out the oxalate vegetables and almonds and my copper levels returned. It took over six months for the peripheral neuropathy to get better but I went from not being able to walk over fifty feet without having to sit down to now being able to walk again with minimal numbness. So remember to check in with your progress, as sometimes the things we think are making us well may not be suiting us any longer and we need to make adjustments.

We don't go out to eat a whole lot because frankly we can eat better at home. I use coconut flour and now minimal almond flour to make spaghetti. I make a mean guacamole (but can't eat restaurant Mexican food since corn and wheat are two staples of that cuisine). I have a great recipe for ice cream. I even make pizza using sheep cheese but it's definitely not like the real thing.

Listen To Your Body

"You are what you eat" is something we all have heard but my experiences and subsequent research has led me to believe there is an absolute connection between food and our body, our nervous system, and indeed all the systems that run our bodies. While I'm certainly not saying my diet is right for everyone—hey, I would for sure be eating cheese and corn tortillas if I could!—the important thing is to listen to what your body is telling you. If I could only go back and tell my younger self that what my doctor was telling me—just add fiber—was not going to help my IBS!

My recommendation is praying and meditating for discernment to connect to God, connecting the dots, and then drawing the conclusion that's appropriate for you. When you sit in prayer or meditation sessions, pay attention to the movement of energy in your body and mind—where it is stuck and where it is flowing. Ask questions about certain foods and certain supplements—about what is right for you—and pay attention to the answers that come in.

And here's another quick story about the curative power of eating only what your body can tolerate.

Before I reworked my diet, I thought I had sleep apnea. I would wake up in the middle of the night and feel like I couldn't breathe. I got myself tested and found I did not have sleep apnea. So what was wrong?

After much inward listening and eliminating "bad" things from my diet, this sleep issue was gone. Totally gone. I now believe my body was going through some inflammatory process in my intestines that caused pressure on my diaphragm, bloating if you will; it was trying to tell me I was ingesting the wrong "fuel."

I had to come to the conclusion that my body simply can't tolerate the same things most people can enjoy. I certainly would love to indulge my foodie self by eating anything and everything—I dream about it—but I know I will pay the price for doing that. And I'm not willing to. As I previously mentioned, somewhere down the line I may "cheat" every now and then—we all deserve cheat days once in a while—but it's more important for me to have my health.

The Challenge of Eating Healthy

There are plenty of restaurants that advertise healthy food or healthy menu choices and lots of so-called healthy options in the supermarket but it should be said that what's healthy for one person may be toxic for another. Plus, there is a difference between eating healthy and eating wholesome. I truly believe that.

Many people rely on supplements instead of getting nutrients from the food they eat. I'm against that except in cases where bloodwork shows supplementation is necessary. You know where a lot of those supplements are manufactured? China. Enough said. I have been to China and could not even breathe the air. So many of these supplements are polluted by toxins, which I realize can also be present in our food. I know by eating organic raw vegetables and fruits I get all the vitamins I need.

As I mentioned before, I infrequently go out to eat now because my diet is so restricted. I used to love going to different restaurants and would never suggest anyone stop doing that—but it is important to know what is going into your body. If you have unexplained aches and pains and a doctor keeps telling you you're fine, think about what you're eating; that might be the culprit.

And I can't end a chapter on food without saying something about excitotoxins, chemicals that cause brain cells to become overexcited and fire uncontrollably, leading to cell death. Many restaurants use excitotoxins in their food, and they are also present in prepackaged foods, spices, and many of the sugar-free, low-fat products people eat in an attempt to be healthier—to amp up the flavor—but they are damaging your brain and your entire body.

Common foods that contain excitotoxins include any with unnatural "flavors" or "flavoring" and anything that is "ultra-pasteurized," "enzyme-modified," "protein-fortified," or fermented. Because excitotoxins stimulate taste buds, they are very attractive to the food industry but their effect on the brain can include migraines, allergies, infections, obesity, and even diseases like Alzheimer's, Parkinson's, and Huntington's.

Yes, you are what you eat. And even though it can be hard to truly eat healthy today, I can tell you from firsthand experience it's worth the effort to discover what foods may be toxic to your body. And of course, try to steer clear of ingredients that are unhealthy for everyone.

And guess what? It's not just what you put in your body you have to be mindful about but also what you put on your skin. Your largest organ absorbs so much of what you put on it. I'm not saying you have to be a granola child and not put on any beauty products whatsoever but look carefully at the ingredients.

When you are very ill it is important to take a look at the whole picture. What could be contributing to your illness? None of this hasn't been said before but perhaps I'm saying it a bit differently. Going within, tuning into God, opened up a plethora of opportunities for me to heal. When I finally let go of listening to everything that didn't make any sense to focus on prayer and completely let go to the faith that my channel connected to God had empirical knowledge for me is when the answers came.

You may not get all the answers right away or ever but if you tune in for long enough, one answer leads to many resolutions. There is no money involved in tuning into your channel with God, there is no gimmick, there is no supplement, there is no pill to take—He is free. It is accessible at any time and no one can take it away from you; He is always within you. God is always with you. God lies within all of us. It is the reason why I have written this book. No one, and I mean no one, knows you better than God. And once you learn to tune in to the gift that has been given to you, have complete faith in it, you gain a sense of empowerment that can change the course of your life.

#10 Witt's Its

- Healing from a life-threatening illness is multifaceted.

- I believe food is one of the most fundamental healing modalities we have. It can kill us, injure us, and nurture us.

- Listen to your inner voice when you're experiencing symptoms that seem to be related to the food you are eating. I listened to my doctors instead of my inner voice (and my body screaming at me) for so long until I finally wised up.

- The mind and body are connected. The brain and gut are connected. If you are suffering from any neurological disorder, any autoimmune disorder, or any illness that involves any of the above it is imperative that you look at your diet.

- Be a skeptic and ask questions. What does it tell you if a doctor is selling a book and also selling supplements—his supplements? Be mindful of what they are trying to sell you, the bill of goods. Is it good for you? Or is it good for them? Supplements are known to have toxic levels of arsenic and other poisons in them. They are minimally regulated.

- When you sit in prayer or meditation sessions, pay attention to the movement of energy in your body and mind—where it is stuck and where it is flowing. Ask questions about what is right for you, and pay attention to the answers that come in.

- Let food be thy medicine—it is the building block, the most foundational structure of your health.

Chapter 11
Lessons Learned And The Road Forward

Many of us spend our entire lives doing the exact opposite of what I espouse in this book. We will do anything—shop, do drugs, pay attention to distractions of all kinds—to not go inward. Why? Because it is excruciatingly painful to observe our truths, especially in difficult times.

To go inward and listen to what God, i.e., our inner voice, says means we must acknowledge our most painful thoughts and emotions. You cannot run away from yourself. That "gut feel" is always there. You just have to tap into it. The gut feel is God speaking to you. Listen.

Once you take the step to sit with yourself, in solitude, you will find immense surrender. It is exhausting to run away from something or someone all the time. You will find over time that you will not be able to go a day without inward prayer and meditation.

As I've said before, the mind and body are connected. When your channel is tuned in the answers come in energy shifts and feelings more than actual words, although not always. When there are zero distractions and no haste, as you begin your journey you will see yourself guided to answers to the questions you ask through those shifts. If you become frustrated, just sit. Breathe. Let it come in another sitting. Do not force.

At the end spend time in gratitude. Just to be able to live another day is an offering. Every day I sit and dial in. Some days my station comes in loud and other days it is barely tuned in. Those are natural ebbs and flows. You may say you don't hear or feel anything. Stop forcing. Surrender to that moment. Breathe and have faith that at that moment this is where you need to be. I believe 100 percent in faith. Believe that at this moment this is what is meant for you.

Part of dialing in is letting go of your will and letting go of your wants. If you surrender to knowing that God is in control and not you, that in and of itself is freeing. You cannot feel and hear what's best through your channel if you are directing and controlling via motives and what you want. In your practice, certainly be mindful that you may want that job or you may want something for yourself—but be mindful of that energy without control. We are human and have wants and needs but do not let that "I have to have this" guide you.

Let go of control as you sit. You will feel a shift in energy as you liberate that energy. Letting go enables the connection to God to move through you. It is acceptance. Acceptance that you are angry, let down, frustrated, or hurt. In that space, clarity is welcomed and silence creates lucidity. And in that state you will dial in God, intuition, your inner voice—however you want to say it. Remember in the spiritual desert when you are truly alone will you find God. His presence is undeniable. Clear and distinct. But for those of you who have not gone through long suffering and have not been in that spiritual desert it is still attainable to connect.

If you tune in regularly, you are making decisions for your greater good most of the time that can ultimately save your life and certainly enhance it and provide deeper, more profound life experiences. Too often, we lose sight that we are guided by God, by intuition, by higher self, since birth. Life, with all its diversions and outward distractions like social media, makes us forget how to have faith and trust that we ultimately know what is best for us. It is not to say as I sit here, I chatted with God and now I will live a long and prosperous life. This is not at all what I profess. God and this universe have plans beyond our control and if that means I am gone tomorrow, so be it. Letting go to that possibility, not morbidly but that the choice is not yours to make, relinquishes all power and control. So many of our fears that drive us today have to do with dying and our final days. When you relinquish this to God, and completely accept he is in control, the fear dissipates. Surrender what you cannot control. Act on faith not on fear. This is something that takes practice daily. Do not let disappointment get you down if this does not come easy, it's not meant to. Continue to practice letting go.

My Wish For You

Although my journey to where I am today has been long, and often frustrating and painful, it has not been without its "silver linings." It is because of this, even though I am a private person, that I want to share my story. It comes from a genuine wish that my experience will help you or anyone with significant health challenges persevere as I have—learning to tune in and regain power through refining the process of listening to God inside of you.

There's not a day that goes by that I don't give thanks to be alive. My life is certainly a lot different than it used to be—I'm minus a few body parts but I'm here. When I think of where I've been and where I am today I can't help but be grateful.

I count my blessings every day, and I have so many of them. But there were many times when I lost sight of that. When you're very, very ill, it's like being in a dust storm—you have no clarity, no sense of what's up or down, no energy, not able to see past the dust in front of you and your ability to process thoughts is just gone. Only once the dust settles are you able to have insight toward what has happened, which is why it is so imperative to go inward in times of crisis—and actually all the time. God is there for you.

Now that I'm on the other side, a changed person getting used to a new way of living, I can reflect on where I was and what aided my ability to carry on and overcome everything that came my way. I've earned my "scars"—I survived. I have scars all over my body and I have invisible scars as well; I am proud of each and every one of them, since they are battle wounds of survival.

Surrender

Anyone who is blessed with good health may not be able to understand the concept of surrender when you think you may be dying. I know it would be hard to wrap my head around it if I hadn't experienced its benefits myself.

When I went through many of my health issues, including cancer, I held onto control. I was constantly thinking about what I could do to get better and often grasping at straws in the process. I truly believe if I had continued down that path, with my body being in a hyper, aggressive state, I would not be in the shape I am in today. It's not to say I am in fantastic shape. One cannot go through so many lethal assaults and come out unscathed. I have many deficits I deal with daily but to use all my energy to hold on to fear and control would not put me where I am today, in a state of healing.

It was in my darkest time, when I was suffering from encephalomeningitis, that I finally decided to let go of the reins, so to speak. When everything was so painful and I had nothing else except that pain, I surrendered. I was in my spiritual desert. That doesn't mean I gave up the will to live but I let go of the will to control and surrendered it to a power larger than me, God, and the will of that power.

The "old me" would have been skeptical, wondering how you can have faith in something you can't see or touch but just feel. But when I was in so much pain and I stopped trying to control the narrative, something radically changed. Part of getting well begins in the moment you let go—the exact opposite of what I'd been doing my entire life is what got me through.

You surrender yourself to God's will. If you don't believe in God, then it is a surrendering to a greater will. It is letting go to what will be. Imagine being in a spiritual place where you don't get the date you want or the job you want and to be able to say, I trust you God; it is not meant for me. It is not to say as a human being you do not feel some disappointment but rather a realization that you are guided and it is not what is meant for you. Believe in spite of not having proof. You don't need theological faith to have faith without certain proof. Whether you think it's unlikely that God or a higher self exists, you are believing that without certain proof anyway. That is faith. When you think about it, my old self believed that nothing created the universe (the Big Bang), which really is just as mind-blowing as believing that God created everything. The choice is yours.

Be Your Own Advocate

After everything I've gone through, I believe we all have the opportunity to choose our own healthcare path. Sure, we may not all be doctors but we know ourselves better than anyone else. I know I said this before but it's worth repeating: when it comes to your physical health, I feel it's important to connect the dots and draw a conclusion.

Now this doesn't mean ignoring the medical community; that is not what I am talking about. It should go without saying that if you keel over from a heart attack that is not the time to go inward—you get yourself to the nearest hospital. If you don't feel well, absolutely go to the doctor, get bloodwork done, check your hormones, get diabetes and thyroid panels—exhaust all the possibilities when it comes to getting a diagnosis, especially if it's a "tricky" disease. And you don't have to rely solely on Western medicine; there are functional doctors or check with a naturopath or a doctor who practices another form of holistic medicine. For me there was no right answer—I tried "all of the above," everything from well-respected Western doctors to spiritual healers. I took a few prescriptions but relied heavily on alternatives like herbs and grasses.

When you are in pain you just want to be fixed. And if you continue to feel bad and are told over and over again by medical professionals they can't find anything wrong with you—as I was—don't give up. Don't let them convince you that you have a psychological problem, "it's all in your head." You may be exhausted, you may need time to regroup—but if your inner voice is telling you there's more, keep looking; you just may not be looking in the right place. Trust me I know—I know how frustrating, how devastating it can be to continue to run into dead ends but do not ever quit. You're allowed to take a break but don't ever stop.

If I had not been my own advocate and continued to press when I knew something was wrong, even after multiple doctors told me otherwise, I would not be here today. I truly believe that.

Look Inward

Today's society makes it so easy for people to become egoists and pay too much attention to their external selves. Just look at social media, which allows us to choose what we want others to see; there are those who portray themselves as victims to get pity and those who showcase their "fabulous" lives to get attention.

All of this focus on the external—trying to manufacture joy and perhaps bury our true selves—is not doing us any favors. And it certainly is of no help during the worst of times. I was forced inward when I had lost sight, sound, and ability—everything except pain—and now I believe wholeheartedly that having an inward focus on your connection with God offers healing we would have otherwise overlooked.

Monks go inward toward nirvana. Christians go inward for prayer. Buddhists, Hindus, all go inward. It is a path toward creativity and certainly toward peace. What I felt in the dark enveloped me; this sense did not come from me and was a divine, ethereal presence.

When you practice tuning in to your station, that doesn't mean all your "stuff" disappears, all your problems are gone. It means you begin to learn what it is you need, even if you didn't realize you needed it. I believe it's a much better alternative than ignoring your innermost thoughts and relying on Egogram posts to showcase what you think the world wants to see and ignore your most pressing problems. Stop feeling this social pressure from these artificial, fake social media lives and concentrate on your own life and goals and needs.

With all the external social media crap out there it is easy to covet others' lives. This is exactly what these tools want to accomplish—you need more, buy more, you're not pretty enough, or whatever. When you are bombarded with these insecurities it is in this moment you should turn it off. When you realize you are coveting a perfect stranger's life, this is the moment to turn this off. You are imperfectly perfect and are in your current space in life where you should be. Trust in that faith and process and enjoy everything you have been blessed with, even the difficult stuff.

Express Gratitude

Gratitude is something that's often undervalued. I've always been grateful for the life I have—a happy marriage, two healthy daughters, a comfortable existence—but it was during some of my most challenging times that I really came to learn the importance of gratitude. It's easy to be grateful when times are good; it's not so easy to be grateful when your whole body hurts, you are in tremendous emotional turmoil, during a divorce, a sickness, or anytime life is difficult. I learned in darkness to try to practice gratitude and see what happens.

In my deepest, darkest times I was bombarded by fear. When we practice gratitude, it is impossible to feel fear. Try it. Take five minutes to count the things you are grateful for. Be specific to your own life.

Every day I take time to think about the things I am grateful for. Even if I'm not feeling well—and trust me, I still do have some bad days—I make an effort to focus on the positive. I truly believe if you choose to look at darkness, you also need to look at light; it's an important yin and yang. If you focus more on darkness, darkness will prevail. If you focus on light, light will prevail. It truly is a choice to make, and what a wonderful choice that is.

Pray For Discernment

I've never been religious but I've been spiritual; you know this if you've read the whole book. But through all my health woes I came to grow my spirituality and develop a strong belief in the power of God and inward healing.

At several times over the years I was ill I actually felt that my life essence was gone. I recall after coming home following my coma, at exactly thirty years old, when I was tethered to an IV line and couldn't even walk to the bathroom without help. I looked in my bathroom mirror and saw no life force in my eyes; they were dull and lifeless—and I was weak and fading. I had a choice: make amends and let go of life or fight for life, inwardly praying and sitting for answers.

It is not fashionable to go within. The world tells you go outward. But going inward saved me. My allotment of prayer is now an hour a day. I set that time aside no matter what is going on in my life. It is priority to keep this relationship healthy and strong.

Part of the process is releasing guilt and knowing our worth as one of God's children. We're all here for a reason. So much focus on Egogram and TikTok, where all we see is others' lives on full display, echoing grandiosity and fakeness can lead to comparing your own life to these inauthentic displays. If you do this, you will form a sense that you are not enough. My life is not that grand, I should be accomplishing more, I should've or could've. Everyone's grandiose egos on full display; everywhere you look it is difficult not to compare. But do not guilt yourself, you are being bombarded in a world full of "look what I have and own" instead of "look at who I am becoming inside." There is not much on these platforms that show inward mindfulness and the value of becoming you. Where's the dollar in that? In a world flooded with these images and videos there is no better time than now to learn this skill. And I believe the innate ability to survive is within all of us. We all have the ability to heal without any special powers—advocating for ourselves, asking God for help, which are really the same thing. Our bodies have an incredible capability to heal.

Going within and tuning in is a lifelong process. The more you do it, the more enlightened with God you become. It takes practice, so do not give up. Your station as I call it is just a metaphor for speaking to God. You may be really out of sync and staticky but in time God and your relationship with Him will come in louder and louder. Have faith. You will see what happens with practice.

Push Forward

During my many health challenges, I was often told I had an incredible attitude by people who didn't know me too well. While I tried to focus on the positive, in my darkest times I did succumb to feelings of worthlessness and bitterness. Being a doer, loving living life and being active when you see the world go by, people living, making memories, and you are stuck in a bed is quite depressing. This sick state wears on the psyche. It is in those moments that you look around and find no matter how resentful you might feel—you must be grateful. You are alive. Although you may not know why, God has kept you here, in this sick, disabled state; you are still here. Let go of the anger and disappointment to focus on your resilience. You are—fill in the blanks. Look at all you have rather than what you do not have.

There were plenty of days when I had to muster so much will to get myself off the couch—but that was part of pushing forward. This process was not pretty; it was filled with plenty of tears, sweat, and even anger. Some days were better than others. I had to realize my growth wasn't linear but went up and down, up and down—somewhat like a rollercoaster. I would wake up one day so thrilled that I was feeling better only to be knocked down the next.

Remember, I was not one to take pain medications. They didn't agree with me at all; I was not trying to be a martyr. I did feel it was important to feel pain to know if I was getting better. I didn't want to mask what was happening to me because there can be such a fine line between healing and pathological pain. I wanted to be able to discern if there was upward movement—celebrating wins like being able to walk for five more minutes on the way to reaching my full potential.

My New Life

My diseases and illnesses ultimately gave me the greatest gift I've known in life. I can affirm that we are guided by God. It's most important relationship I have to date. If we listen, He will give us the answers we seek. We are not meant to have answers to the divinity and laws of the universe but we are meant to have answers for what is best for us. You always hear people say, oh darn it, I should've listened to my gut instinct. I should've listened to my intuition.

There was no way I was going to come out unscathed after everything I went through. Many have died from just one of the health challenges I overcame. I'm so grateful God has given me more time and I take nothing for granted. Am I healed? Possibly. Who knows for certain. But I still struggle with a lot of things after everything my body has gone through.

I do not see a doctor regularly but I still have many woes and pains. As I said before, I consider them scars. You earn scars and should be proud of them. You fought and you won. Scars are victories won. I have many.

My eyes were gravely affected by so much of what I've been through so I only drive short distances. Having a brain injury, I still have a problem with stimulus so I do not go to places like loud restaurants—for this reason plus I'm so limited by what I can eat. I don't have the same energy level as I had before I was so ill. But I'm talking and walking—two to three miles a day. I have a regimented diet that is healing my body and while I sometimes lament the foods I love but can no longer enjoy, I feel much better on my new diet. I'm embracing my new reality.

I'm focused on enjoying life, doing the things that bring me joy. And one important thing that's changed for me: I don't worry about having everything taken away from me. And I don't ask myself questions I don't have the answer to.

I said this before but it's worth repeating: None of us goes through life unscathed. There are serious challenges we all must overcome—and some of us have been given more challenges than others. Why? No one knows the answer. As I've already noted, no one is privy to the divine laws of the universe and thus knows why some of us suffer more than others. There are so many theories and ideas floated as to why but that's all they are, theories. Have you heard this one? Babies die young because they made past mistakes and wrongs in a past life and are now paying for it in this life—WTF? Or you were an awful human being in a past life and therefore are paying the wrongs in this life? These charlatans are usually selling some sort of gadget, power, or trickery. No one knows this. These are bogus theories to give people answers to questions only God knows.

"Why me?" is something those of us with serious life-threatening illnesses tend to ask ourselves. I believe that question will be answered when we move on from this life. Only God knows the answer. No one else. Until then, it is best to focus on questions you can get answers to.

I believe at birth you are given this gift, living life, but its constant distractions cause diversion and interference: static. Essentially living life causes static but when in tune, you realize you are not alone in making the "right" decision for yourself. You have never been alone. Be patient. You have been on this Earth for many years so you should not expect complete guidance, i.e., tuning in, right away. Let go to the process and accept it is just that—a process. It is practicing discernment, which takes time.

Sitting and tuning into your station is called praying for discernment for a reason. Have faith that you are guided by God. This ability lies in every single one of us. You will feel secure about the future, acceptance, and inner harmony in letting go to God. I share this with you so you can also know the greatest gift I have ever been given in my entire life. I was stubborn and it took over five near-death experiences to finally have faith in God's existence. What can I say, I'm a slow learner. God kept saying, "are you listening?" and my heart was not open to Him. It is now. I also want this gift for you. I want you to know you are not alone. You have never been alone.

#11 Witt's Its

- Make time to tune in—at least three times a week—sitting quietly without hurry in prayer and inward meditation.
- Begin with setting an intention. What are you seeking the answers to? What is in your heart or on your mind? Ask and then let go.
- We lose sight that we are guided by God since birth. Life, with all its diversions and outward distractions like social media, makes us forget how to have faith and trust that we ultimately know what is best for us.
- My diseases and illnesses ultimately gave me the greatest gift I've known in life. I can affirm that we are guided by God, a higher self, intuition. If we listen, He will give us the answers we seek. We are not meant to have answers to the divinity and laws of the universe but we are meant to have answers for what is best for us. You always hear people say, oh darn it, I should've listened to my gut instinct. I should've listened to my intuition.
- That "gut feel" is always there. You just have to tap into it.
- If you tune in regularly, you are making decisions for your greater good most of the time that can ultimately save your life and certainly enhance it and provide deeper, more profound life experiences.
- Letting it go to trust in God will ultimately bring about security, acceptance, and inner harmony.

Photos

Finding Brendan in Roosevelt Field Shopping Mall in New York.

Brendan and our girls in 2005.

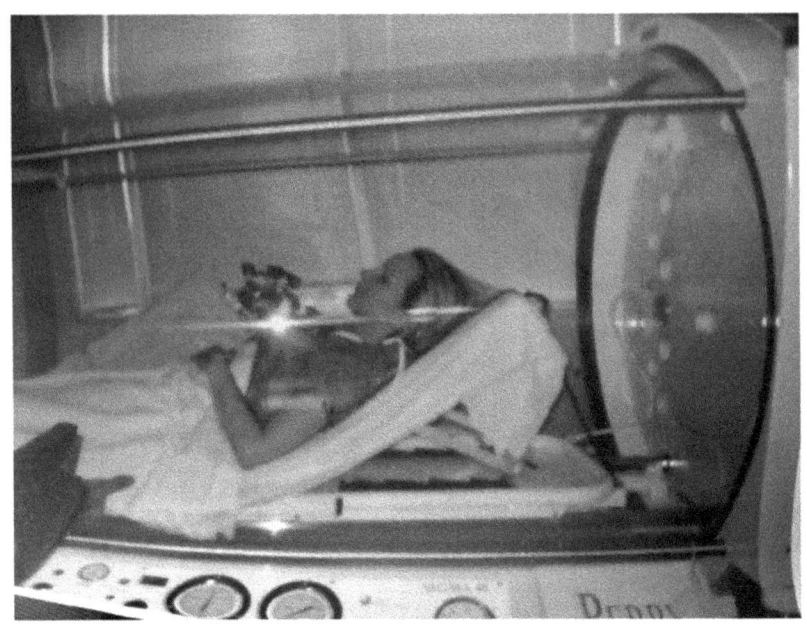

This is me inside the hyperbaric chamber in 2011.

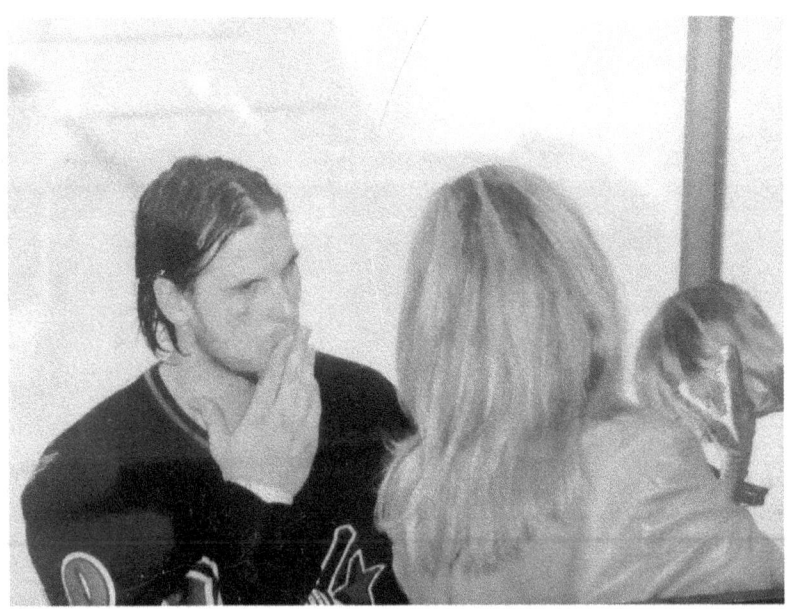

Love from the ice.

The children with cancer were some of the bravest I knew. I had these kids in the locker room until 11 P.M. One boy, named Nicholas Marriam, became close to us and Brendan shaved his head to support him. Nicholas ended up starting his own non-profit called The Nickleby Project, for children with cancer.

The McGowans, a family we met through Witter's Hitters, had three kids with cystic fibrosis. This photo was taken at a Witter's Hitters event just one week before their son, John (center) passed away.

Aliana making her TV debut with Brendan on a local sports show. She was a little camera shy.

Me and Cafe Olé competing in the Sunday Classic at Wellington in Florida.

Brendan with our Beloved Honey.

Making tall memories with family. (2007)

The beauty of nature with family. (2024)

Acknowledgments

Where would I be without my anchor, Brendan? You have made my dreams a reality and the hellish nightmares survivable. I would be lost without your enduring love and support. You have been my rock through all we have been through.

Aliana and Safiya, as your mom I always tried to shelter you from the illnesses I was suffering through when you were young. In your young adulthood you were propelled into a position where you could have bailed and left. Instead, you jumped in and were right there for your dad during the times I was bedridden. You have been my hope when all felt lost. I love you tremendously.

Adrienne Moch, this book would not be a book if it wasn't for you. Thank you for your patience and tolerating my inability to type while I healed—plus your uncanny ability to understand my scribbles. You have a sixth sense and I am forever grateful for your fortitude.

Kathryn Cloward, you galloped into my life at just the right time. Thank you for your generosity of spirit and all the effort and energy you put into helping me ensure my vision for this book was realized.

Dr. Frank and Sandy Ruscetti, thank you for your genuine caring and loving nature to help those of us in need. You are the definition of selfless and two of the world's most brilliant minds. I feel honored to call you both my friends. You steadfastly put others' needs in front of your own and I am forever grateful for your considerate and generous spirits.

To my closest friends, Rick, Jill, and Michaela, thank you for being there. Thank you for picking up the phone, for driving over, for the love and support. Your friendship and love held me up during the darkest times.

www.ingramcontent.com/pod-product-compliance
Lightning Source LLC
Chambersburg PA
CBHW070448050426
42451CB00015B/3386